I Wasn't Ready to Say Goodbye

surviving, coping and healing
after the sudden death of a loved one

A COMPANION WORKBOOK

BY BROOK NOEL WITH PAMELA D. BLAIR, PH.D.

CHAMPION PRESS, LTD.
FREDONIA, WISCONSIN

ISBN: 1891400509
LCCN: 2003092155

Manufactured in the United States of America 20 19 18 17 16 15 14 13 12

VISIT WWW.GRIEFSTEPS.COM
FOR BEREAVEMENT SUPPORT
7 DAYS A WEEK

HOSTED BY BROOK NOEL

ALSO BY BROOK NOEL AND PAMELA D. BLAIR:
I WASN'T READY TO SAY GOODBYE: SURVIVING, COPING AND HEALING AFTER THE SUDDEN DEATH OF A LOVED ONE

ALSO BY BROOK NOEL:
BACK TO BASICS: 101 IDEAS FOR STRENGTHENING OUR CHILDREN AND OUR FAMILIES
THE SINGLE PARENT RESOURCE
THE RUSH HOUR COOK SERIES
GRIEFSTEPS: 10 STEPS TO RECOVER, REBUILD AND RENEW AFTER ANY LIFE LOSS
GRIEFSTEPS: 10 STEPS TO RECOVER, REBUILD AND RENEW AFTER ANY LIFE LOSS WORKBOOK

ALL AVAILABLE AT WWW.CHAMPIONPRESS.COM

CONTENTS

Chapter One
Our Stories

**"What we call the beginning is often the end.
To make an end is to make a beginning.
The end is where we start from."
—T.S. Eliot**

Pam's Story

I believe no matter how much pain we're in, there is something inside of us stronger than the pain. That something allows survivors of the worst tragedies to want to live and tell their story. You can see it in the eyes of someone who has managed to hang on to their dignity in the midst of adversity. It's a kind of stubbornness. You can call it God, the soul or the human spirit. It is found only when we have been oppressed, or broken, or abandoned, and we remain the one who holds on to what's left. It is this inner something that has allowed me to go on in the face of tremendous loss.

I remember all the vivid, surrealistic details of that morning. The smell of fresh ground coffee brewing lingered in the air as I came to consciousness. I was trying to squeeze one or two more minutes out of warm bed and feather pillow when the phone rang. Grabbing at the intrusive noise, I put the receiver to my ear and heard nothing but the sound of someone trying to catch her breath. I thought it might be one of those weird "breather" calls until I heard LeAnne say, "Pam, George is in a coma.....(long pause).....he had a hemorrhage or something." I felt the molecules in the air begin to thicken as I tried to take a breath so I could talk to George's younger sister. "LeAnne, where are you? What do you mean? I just saw George yesterday afternoon. He looked fine!"

Crying and gasping for air she replied in a thin voice, "You and Ian have to come here—to the hospital. I think it's important that you bring Ian here now." I tried to remain rational as I remembered that Ian, my twelve-year-old son with George, was getting ready to bolt down the stairs on his way to school. I still needed to get up and pack his lunch box. I thought, *Why is LeAnne bothering me with this? I'm sure it's just nothing. After all, George is young and healthy (and handsome). Comas don't happen to people like him. They don't happen to people I know.*

"LeAnne, why don't we wait and see. He'll probably come to. And besides, Ian is just about to leave for school and he has a test today. Why don't you call back in a few minutes after you have more information and I'll bring him down to the hospital later. It's probably not as bad as . . ." She interrupted my rambling with a bold, deliberate, almost cold intonation in her voice. "*Now.* You have to come now. It's really bad. There's a lot of blood in his brain and he probably won't live."

1

Blood in his brain. I sat down hard. What was I hearing? Was I hearing that George, the man I had loved as my husband and the father of my child, and who had become a dear friend and loving co-parent after our divorce, was about to leave the earth? Come on. People exaggerate. LeAnne is exaggerating. After all, George means as much to her as he does to me, and his son Ian, and his once step-daughter, Aimee.

"Okay, LeAnne, I'll take the day off from work and I'll bring Ian to the hospital. Where are you?" She replied in an almost inaudible voice, "The emergency room. I'll meet you there."

My limbs were numb, the blood was gone from my face and neck, and I wasn't sure I could make my mouth work. Steve, my husband of seven years had left for his office in the city and I was alone. I would have to tell Ian myself. I would have to tell Ian that the dad who loved to be with him on weekends, who lived for his son's little league games and karate matches was probably brain dead. I would have to tell my daughter, Aimee. Part of me thought that if I could just see George and tell him loudly how much his son needed him, he wouldn't slip away into death's darkness. That's it. I would scream at him and bring him back to us.

Somehow I made my legs work. One numb foot in front of the other. At the bottom of the stairs I called, "Ian, meet me in my bedroom. I have something to tell you." I kept telling myself, *you will remain calm . . .think logically . . .don't upset the boy too much, just keep calm.*

How do you describe this strange limbo moment where life slows down and everything around you falls away into unimportance? It felt like there was no house with its comfortable furniture around me, no more smell of coffee, no cat rubbing my legs for attention, no appointments on the calendar—all that existed for now were the two small, brown, round eyes of my little boy resting on mine.

I told Ian what little I knew. There, sitting on the edge of my now neatly made bed, he melted into tears. Deep sobs and a lot of "How did this happen? What happened to him?" over and over again. His voice was cracking, rising and falling, the way twelve-year-old boy's voices sometimes do. I comforted him. I knew that was my only role, comforter to my son with no one to comfort me.

I called my daughter Aimee, nine months pregnant with her first child and George's stepdaughter. She agreed to join us. We made our way to the hospital, not talking. Ian looked out the car window and I could tell he wondered why everyone driving past us looked so normal, so unaffected by our plight. Didn't they know what was going on? How could they go about their business knowing George was dying *or dead*? Why are they behaving as if nothing happened? I felt as if I were moving through someone else's movie. Everything felt surreal, in slow motion.

No human being is without feelings. From a baby's first cry to a dying person's last look at friends and family, our primary response to the world around us is colored by emotion. Whether that world seems to us friendly or frightening, beautiful or ugly, pleasant or disagreeable, affects the way we approach others, and indeed influences everything we do. I do not believe that such feelings arise in us solely due to environmental conditions, or to genetic factors, however important these both may be. Members of the same family, placed in the same kinds of situations, react in very different ways. Our emotions are a conscious response to our experience, but they are self-generated and reveal something important about our character.

It felt like I had no emotions and no character that day. I was skin and bones and brain and blood vessels making attempts at movement. Lips in slow motion on a frozen face with unfamiliar arms and legs, a mind repeating over and over, *this is crazy, this is crazy*. George's mother and sister waited with Ian, Aimee and I in the emergency room. We all looked the same as we did last week only now we were more robot-like, sitting and standing and walking and pacing around a room with hard plastic chairs and a TV set hanging from the ceiling. I couldn't look at George's mom with her soft round face and gray hair. A gentle lady of 62 with kind blue eyes—the same kind blue eyes that George had. If I looked at her I would have seen the pain. The pain of a woman who was told she would probably never have children and to whom George was a miracle, a gift from God—her first-born.

To me, the emotions are "real" in the sense that I can perceive them objectively as a luminous atmosphere surrounding every living being. Every time we feel an emotion there is a discharge of energy in the emotional field, whether slight or strong, and this produces a characteristic vibration and a color—the "footprint" of that particular emotion. I could "see" the emotion in the room.

George was brain dead. The doctor said he had suffered a massive cerebral aneurysm. He was dead and he looked like he was sleeping—the machines kept his lungs rising and falling, his heart beating, his face a rosy healthy glow. I encouraged Ian to hold his hand, to say goodbye. He was brave. He did. He cried and said, "Goodbye, Daddy, I love you." Aimee took her private moment with him also. George had, only the week before, stopped by to visit her in her new apartment, to place his hand on her baby-full belly, to say congratulations.

George's wife said I could have some time alone with him. Because I believe that people in comas can "hear," I told him "thank you for our son and for the love you showed Aimee. Thank you for the time we had together." I think he heard me, if not with his ears, with his soul. I asked him to please be an angel in our son's life—to watch over him. The hospital staff began disconnecting the machines as the family encircled the hospital bed, holding hands and praying.

I tell my story because I believe in the power of story to heal. As a therapist and workshop leader, I find it rewarding to help others tell their story. The stories I hear about loss are as diverse as fingerprints—each one slightly different from the next. And yet, when we gather like we did at a recent workshop I conducted, the attendees share and the connection to each other is immediate and profound. Regardless of where we are in the process of loss we become supportive as we relate and recognize each others pain. A sense of community and acceptance is vital to our spiritual and emotional healing.

In her book, *The Fruitful Darkness*, Buddhist anthropologist and depth psychologist Joan Halifax reflects on our collective as well as personal stories when she writes, "stories are our protectors, like our immune system, defending against attacks of debilitating alienation...They are the connective tissue between culture and nature, self and other, life and death, that sew the worlds together, and in telling, the soul quickens and comes alive."

3

In his classic book, *Reaching Out*, Henri Nouwen writes that though our own story "can be hard to tell, full of disappointments and frustrations, deviations and stagnations...it is the only story we have and there will be no hope for the future when the past remains unconfessed, unreceived and misunderstood."

Hopefully, the stories and information in this workbook will help you feel less alone as you struggle to find the path that will lead you across rivers of grief and through forests of sadness. We hope in some small way that we can be your support network and a touchstone for sanity during a very difficult time.

Brook's Story

It was a day in October that changed my perception of life, and my perception of death, forever. It was the day I lost my brother, who was not only a brother, but in many ways a father, a friend and a lifeline.

The day was unseasonably warm for a Wisconsin October. It was the fourth of the month and the thermometer showed a temperature near seventy degrees. With weather like that, no Wisconsinite would stay indoors. My husband, daughter and I decided to take a trip to Manitowoc, a town about an hour north of our then-home-base in the Milwaukee suburbs. Manitowoc housed a Maritime Museum that we had yet to visit. The main feature was a submarine, complete with tour. That afternoon we walked the streets, looked in the shops, took the tour, and bought our two and a half-year-old daughter a blue hat, which read U.S.S. Cobia. Our daughter posed with the hat, her smile radiating happiness.

We left Manitowoc around five that evening to return home. A dear friend of mine had traveled into town and we had plans to meet at six for dinner. I glanced at my watch as we continued the drive, knowing I would be a few minutes late. The plan was that she leave a message with where she was and I would meet her there. We didn't get home until a little bit after six. My neighbors, Kevin and Mary Ann were outside barbecuing. I stopped over briefly to say hello and let Samantha show off her new hat. I apologized for my quick departure and ducked into the house to check messages and find out where Sara had chosen for dinner.

The red digital display showed four messages. I hit play. The first was from my mother. It said simply to call her right away. The second was from Sara, with the name of the restaurant. The third was from my mother again, this time her voice sounding thick with a tone I couldn't discern, "Brook you must call me right away. There's been a terrible accident." I immediately pushed stop on the machine and dialed my mother's number. Both my brother and mother continued to live in the town where I was raised. It's a small resort town called Manitowish Waters, about five hours north of my then-Milwaukee home. Life is simple there. You work; you ski; you enjoy the woods, the lakes; you "watch the Packers" and enjoy the seasons as they unfold. Outsiders make great attempts to vacation there. Often the northwoods has been dubbed "God's Country", and life is full and fun there.

My mother answered on the first ring. I can still hear our voices to this day and picture myself standing beneath the archway of our guest bedroom. "Mom, it's me. What's up?" I asked inquisitively, never prepared for the two-word response that would vibrate over the phone.

"Caleb's dead."

Immediately my knees gave out beneath me as I shouted "No," before falling to the floor, the questions, the disbelief, lingering around me. I asked how, but did not hear the reply. I crawled into the guest bed with the cordless phone pushed to my ear and curled my body into a tight ball. I could do nothing but sob. My daughter had walked up behind me and was patting me gently on the back. "It's all right Mama," said the innocent two-year-old voice. "It's all right Mama." Andy, my husband, came and took Samantha from the room and I simply mouthed the words my mother had said, *Caleb's dead*.

My mother suggested that I hang up the phone and call her back. I put down the phone while I still writhed on the bed, wanting desperately to escape from the unwelcome reality that had suddenly become claustrophobic. Rising, I walked into the living room. I looked briefly at my daughter and Andy, before running from the house. The points thereafter are somewhat vague and gathered mostly from what I've been told of my response.

I entered into my neighbor's kitchen and fell into her arms as I told her the news. She quickly took me outside and huddled me close. All I remember is her telling me, "You are in shock." I remember my hands trembling violently and my body shaking. Her husband got Samantha from our house to play with their children; and then she and my husband Andy called my mother.

The details unfurled. Caleb and his faithful chocolate lab Samson, had been duck hunting out on a marsh with three friends. They had rowed a boat out about 20 minutes to the site that was thought to have the best potential. While waiting for the official opening time, Caleb was eyeing some geese that were flying over. At that moment he was stung by a yellow jacket just over his eyebrow. Within minutes, Caleb would go unconscious. His friends performed CPR as they frantically rowed back to shore. Unable to fit in the boat, his faithful dog swam across the marsh, unwilling to leave his master. His friends broke into his truck, using his cellular phone to call the paramedics. The local paramedics arrived and were then intercepted by a special team sent from the hospital that was about thirty miles away.

Despite the efforts of friends, paramedics and doctors, Caleb never came to nor responded to Epinephrine or any other drug. My mother was told he had suffered a fatal, profound anaphylactic shock reaction to the sting of a bee. Caleb had been stung by bees before and never had 'but a mild reaction. We, nor he, even knew of this bee allergy.

My brother was a strong and vital young man. He owned a successful printing shop, which he built from the ground up. He was a National Barefoot Water-ski Champion who was in great physical health and a prime athlete. He was about 200 pounds, and in one day, we had to come to understand that a bee, no bigger than an inch, had taken the life from this handsome twenty-seven-year-old man. It is something that I think we all are still trying to comprehend. It is something that I don't think we ever

5

fully will, but we each must find our own way to cope and go on successfully—that is the best tribute we can give to this great man who touched our lives.

When Caleb died, I looked for someone to hold my hand and to understand what I was feeling. I wasn't ready for a support group, all I wanted to do was to curl up in my bed, hide from the world and have something convince me it would, some day, be all right again. I scanned bookstores looking for something I could relate to but found very little coverage on sudden death. The other books didn't understand the unique challenges of facing a death in this way. Eventually, I gave up the search for that book.

As time has passed, I have learned more about what I have endured and what I have to endure to move on with my life. I have spoken with others—some in the recent aftermath and some who lost someone tragically years ago—many of whom are looking for guidance similar to what I had searched for. With these people in mind, I decided to create the book I wish would have been there for me. I met my coauthor, Pam, while working on a book entitled *The Single Parent Resource*. There was an immediate closeness between the two of us, even though we lived two-thousand miles apart. When I decided to write this book, I felt compelled to call her and see if she would consider writing the book with me. Fate must have nudged me to call, since at that point, I didn't know she had experienced sudden loss in her life as well.

We cannot offer you any quick fixes. We cannot give you a tidy outline that will divide grief recovery into a neat and precise process. We cannot tell you that six months from now the world will be back in alignment. We have seen too much to offer such hollow promises. What we can promise, is that in these pages we will do our best to offer you a hand to hold and words to guide you through your maze, so that you may come out complete and hopeful on the other side.

Chapter Two
The First Few Weeks

"And people answered the phone for me. And people cooked for me. And people understood for me. My dearest friends cared for me when I didn't care." —Wendy Feiereisen

At this moment, in the direct aftermath of losing someone tragically, there is so little anyone can say. We cannot find the words to offer you peace—though we wish it a gift we could give you. We promise you now that we will give you everything we can to help you make your way through this. Throughout this workbook, we will help you wind a path through the haze, the confusion and the pain.

For the first few weeks, do not concern yourself with what you will do, where you will go or what lies in the future. For now, we ask that you simply follow the guidelines in this chapter. There will be time to cope, to understand, to process—later. Right now, you simply need to take care of *you*.

Treat Yourself as if You Were in Intensive Care

You are in the process of going through one of the most traumatic experiences a person can endure. The challenges you have already faced, both physically and mentally, will leave you vulnerable, exhausted and weak. It's imperative that you focus directly on yourself and on any dependents. In the following worksheet, we identify your most basic needs. Keep your focus just on the needs we identify for the near future.

If you have small children, contact friends and relatives to help you care for them. Consider having someone stay with you for the specific task of caring for your children since some children may be further traumatized by separation. A bit later we will cover how to specifically help children. While it is human nature to want to help and care for others, we must understand at this trying time we will barely have enough energy to care for ourselves. Even if we want to help those around us, we won't have the resources. It's in our best interest to allow this time for our own grief. Have a friend help you complete the following worksheet to narrow down the things that must be done during these first few weeks.

Your Immediate Needs

Children

Who can help care for your children? Even when you are present, you will likely be occupied with your own grief. This is perfectly normal. Do not try to "do it all". Instead, create a list of people who can help by being present to offer additional support to your children.

Monday	Support Person	Phone Number
_____	_____	_____
Tuesday	Support Person	Phone Number
_____	_____	_____
Wednesday	Support Person	Phone Number
_____	_____	_____
Thursday	Support Person	Phone Number
_____	_____	_____
Friday	Support Person	Phone Number
_____	_____	_____
Saturday	Support Person	Phone Number
_____	_____	_____
Sunday	Support Person	Phone Number
_____	_____	_____

Are there any other support people available that your children should know about?

_____

_____

_____

_____

_____

_____

_____

_____

_____

Your Support System

Who can you call if you need support or assistance?

_____

_____

_____

_____

_____

School and Work

Has your employer been contacted and notified of any time you will need away from work?

Employer's Name   **Employer's Number**

_____

Has your child's school been contacted and notified of any time needed away from school, or any special assistance needed for other children?

School's Name   **School's Number**

_____

Have a friend help make these calls if you are not up to it.

Are there any urgent or pressing bills or claims that need to be filed in the next couple of weeks?

☐ Mortgage or Rent   Contact Information _____
☐ Other Loan Payments   Contact Information _____
☐ Insurance   Contact Information _____
☐ Car Payments   Contact Information _____
☐ Life Insurance   Contact Information _____
☐ Accounts Payable   Contact Information _____
☐ CCD'S   Contact Information _____
☐ Taxes   Contact Information _____
☐ Other   Contact Information _____
☐ Other   Contact Information _____
☐ Other   Contact Information _____

A Checklist of Calls to Make

Below you will find other calls that need to be made. Let your support people help or make these calls for you. Discuss them with your support person before they call. If this list is overwhelming at the moment, come back to it later or let your support team bring relevant calls to your attention.

☐ Call a support person to help you. Give the support person this list and let them work through it and ask questions as necessary.

☐ Choose a funeral home to assist in arrangements. Set date and time for funeral and memorial services.
Funeral Home Name _____ Phone Number _____
ContactPerson _____

☐ Contact the newspaper for the obituary.

☐ Choose a memorial or charity for any gifts or donations. Ask family members and friends of your loved one what ideas and groups they would suggest. Request more information from any groups you would like to learn more about.
Selected Group _____
Contact Information _____
_____

Depending upon your relationship to the deceased, you may need to also make the following calls

☐ Notify all insurance companies—social security, credit union, trade union, fraternal, military, standard life, credit card, etc. Check for income from any of these sources as well.

☐ Call all debtors in a timely manner. Insurance may cancel out some debts. For other debts ask for a payment plan.

☐ If the deceased lived alone, contact the landlord and utilities. Select a group of people to help move the deceased's belongings from the apartment/home.

☐ Contact a lawyer and the executor of the will, if a will is in place. If there is no will, contact a lawyer for guidance.

Who Needs to Be Notified

Make a list of people who need to be notified. Try to obtain the deceased's address book for phone numbers and people that might otherwise be overlooked. You may also choose to share this page with friends and other family members. They may have other useful suggestions.

Contacted	Name	Phone Number

Call Log

If the person that has died is of your immediate family, you will be receiving many phone calls, visitors and cards. Have a friend come by to take messages, answer the door and answer the phone. Most callers do not expect to speak directly with the family but simply wish to express their condolences. Have someone log your incoming calls on the log below. You can return them if you like, although don't feel obligated to do so.

Name and Phone Number	Message

Delivering A Eulogy

You may use this worksheet to create a Eulogy or provide it to the person whom you would like to deliver the Eulogy. According to Terence B. Foley and Amanda Bennett (*In Memoriam*, Simon & Schuster, 1997), "The most important thing to remember when delivering a eulogy is that it is a gift. A gift for you to be able to speak about a family member or friend before those who also loved and respected him...It is not a performance, nor will it be judged as such. Your job is to be thoughtful and genuine..."

This form should get you thinking about those things that were most important about the deceased. As you deliver the eulogy, do not rush, take your time. If you decide to use humor, make sure it is done with affection. Avoid jokes and stories that would embarrass those present. If you lose your composure, give yourself a moment of quiet, take a deep breath or a drink of water, and go on.

My relationship with the deceased:

_____

_____

I've known him/her for how long:

_____

_____

How we met:

_____

_____

_____

_____

What I remember most...

_____

_____

_____

_____

Positive Qualities:

_____

_____

_____

_____

What was eccentric about them (presented with affection):

_____

_____

_____

_____

Kindnesses I received from the deceased:

_____

_____

_____

_____

What would the deceased say about the events today:

_____

_____

_____

_____

_____

_____

Integrating what we learned from this person into our own lives is a constant memorial and source of comfort for the family. Therefore, consider the following three questions:

What did I learn from this person (through example or teaching):

_____

_____

_____

_____

How do I plan to implement what I learned from them:

_____

_____

_____

_____

What words of wisdom would the deceased want us to remember:

_____

_____

_____

_____

NOTES:

_____

_____

_____

_____

When honoring a loved one, go with what feels intuitively right to you. What touches you deeply will likely touch others. When Brook was in her teens, she lost a friend in a car accident. At the service, the friend's father got up to speak. Barely able to get the words out between gasps and tears, he delivered a few minutes that moved everyone in the room. The deceased was a performer and he ended his talk with, "Always a performer, let's give him one more standing ovation for the time he gave us." Everyone in the room stood, clapping with all their might, tears streaming down their faces as they honored their friend. Typical? No. But it moved everyone more than any other spoken words could have.

Naturally, the best way to honor a friend is to speak from the heart—your heart. What you say doesn't have to be eloquent or full of fancy epitaphs. Simple, straightforward and heartfelt words are what the family is longing to hear. Again, there is really no right or wrong way to eulogize a friend. You can sing a song, write a poem, dance a dance or read what someone else has written. Use your imagination and trust your instincts. If you are intuitively drawn to a particular reading or creative act, it may even be your friend who is gently nudging you, instructing you on how to celebrate his life.

NOTES:

_____

_____

_____

_____

_____

_____

_____

_____

_____

_____

_____

_____

The Memorial Service

When the person in charge of the memorial service does not know the deceased, consider filling out this form and giving it to them. Keep a copy for yourself. The information included on the form will be an aid in creating a meaningful service. This form will be equally helpful even if the person in charge knew your loved one.

If at all possible, do not fill out this form alone. Ask friends and family to contribute information. If your loved one had a career, chances are they have a resume in a file somewhere. Their resume may help fill in some of the blanks.

INFORMATION TO PROVIDE TO THE PERSON (OR CLERGY) IN CHARGE :

Name of deceased: Age:

Cause of death: Date of birth:

Religious background (if any):   Date of death:

Type of service the deceased would have liked (i.e. quiet, casual, formal, offbeat):

Those who would like to participate:

Family background:

Education:

Career (or career aspirations):

Club memberships or affiliations:

Activities or hobbies:

Relationships:

What kind of books did he or she read?

What were his or her dreams?

What was he or she most proud of?

Who were his or her friends, family?

What kind of music did he or she enjoy?

Favorite bible verse or inspirational verse:

Favorite poet or poems:

Favorite charity/charities:

NOTES:

_____

_____

_____

_____

_____

_____

_____

_____

_____

_____

_____

_____

_____

_____

_____

_____

_____

_____

The Power of Friends

If possible, choose a close friend to keep near you through the first week or two. Let this person help you make decisions, hear your fears or concerns and be the shoulder for you to lean on. Give them a copy of this book. Later as you move through the grieving process it will be very helpful to have someone who has "been there" and understands what you are talking about thoroughly.

Our energy is so depleted in the first few weeks after loss, it's hard to even ask for help. We have included a handout, on the next page, that can be photocopied freely and given to your inner circle of friends and relatives. You may be reluctant to do this, but please do. Even when we don't think we need people right now, we do indeed.

The following two entries summarize beautifully what those who face grief need from the people around them:

> "'I'll cry with you,'
> she whispered,
> 'until we run out of tears.
> Even if it's forever.
> We'll do it together.'
> There it was...a simple
> promise of connection.
> The loving alliance of
> grief and hope that
> blesses both our breaking
> apart and our coming
> together again."
> —**Molly Fumia**, *Safe Passage*

"Needed: A strong, deep person wise enough to allow me to grieve in the depth of who I am, and strong enough to hear my pain without turning away.

I need someone who believes that the sun will rise again, but who does not fear my darkness. Someone who can point out the rocks in my way without making me a child by carrying me. Someone who can stand in thunder and watch the lightning and believe in a rainbow." **—Fr. Joe Mahoney, *Concerns of Police Survivors Newsletter***

(This is excerpted from a beautiful book on grief titled Forever Remembered: Cherished messages of hope, love and comfort from courageous people who have lost a loved one. Compendium Publishing.)

A Guide for Those Helping Others with Grief
(photocopy and give to close friends and loved ones)

Don't try to find the magic words or formula to eliminate the pain. Nothing can erase or minimize the painful tragedy your friend or loved one is facing. Your primary role at this time is simply "to be there". Don't worry about what to say or do, just be a presence that the person can lean on when needed.

Don't try to minimize or make the person feel better. When we care about someone, we hate to see them in pain. Often we'll say things like, "I know how you feel," or "perhaps, it was for the best," in order to miminize their hurt. While this can work in some instances, it never works with grief.

Help with responsibilities. Even though a life has stopped, life doesn't. One of the best ways to help is to run errands, prepare food, take care of the kids, do laundry and help with the simplest of maintenance.

Don't expect the person to reach out to you. Many people say, "call me if there is anything I can do." At this stage, the person who is grieving will be overwhelmed at the simple thought of picking up a phone. If you are close to this person, simply stop over and begin to help. People need this but don't have the energy to ask.

Talk through decisions. While working through the grief process many bereaved people report difficulty with decision making. Be a sounding board for your friend or loved one and help them think through decisions.

Don't be afraid to say the name of the deceased. Those who have lost someone usually speak of them often, and believe it or not, need to hear the deceased's name and stories. In fact, many grievers welcome this.

Excerpted from "I Wasn't Ready to Say Good-bye: a guide for surviving, coping and healing after the sudden death of a loved one" by Brook Noel and Pamela D. Blair, Ph.D. (Champion Press, 2000)

Remember that time does not heal all wounds. Your friend or loved one will change because of what has happened. Everyone grieves differently. Some will be "fine" and then experience their true grief a year later, others grieve immediately. There are no timetables, no rules—be patient.

Remind the bereaved to take care of themselves. Eating, resting and self-care are all difficult tasks when beseiged by the taxing emotions of grief. You can help by keeping the house stocked with healthy foods that are already prepared or easy-to-prepare. Help with the laundry. Take over some errands so the bereaved can rest. However, do not push the bereaved to do things they may not be ready for. Many grievers say, "I wish they would just follow my lead." While it may be upsetting to see the bereaved withdrawing from people and activities— it is normal. They will rejoin as they are ready.

Avoid judging. Don't tell the person how to react or handle their emotions or situation. Simply let him/her know that you support their decisions and will help in any way possible.

Share a Meal. Invite the bereaved over regularly to share a meal or take a meal to their home since meal times can be especially lonely. Consider inviting the bereaved out on important dates like the one-month anniversay of the death, the deceased's birthday, etc.

Make a list of everything that needs to be done with the bereaved. This could include everything from bill paying to plant watering. Prioritize these by importance. Help the bereaved complete as many tasks as possible. If there are many responsibilities, find one or more additional friends to support you.

Make a personal commitment to help the one grieving get through this. After a death, many friendships change or disintegrate. People don't know how to relate to the one who is grieving or they get tired of being around someone who is sad. Vow to see your frriend or loved one through this, to be their anchor in their darkest hour.

Excerpted from "I Wasn't Ready to Say Good-bye: a guide for surviving, coping and healing after the sudden death of a loved ones" by Brook Noel and Pamela D. Blair, Ph.D. (Champion Press, 2000)

Chapter Three
Difficult Emotions

"When people ask me what I was feeling... I didn't know how to respond. I wasn't feeling any one emotion—I was feeling everything— all at the same time." —Anonymous

At some point in our grief work, we are likely to find ourselves recounting the days with our loved one in our minds. We may also play out different scenarios of the death, trying to understand what has happened. For some, the review completely preoccupies the mind, and despite our wishes we can think of nothing else.

As is the case with post traumatic stress disorder, you may find yourself living and reliving the experiences you had with your loved one during the days, hours or minutes just before the death occurred. "If only I had not taken that road...If only I had said 'don't go...' If only I had been there I might have prevented the accident..." and on and on.

As you read this, what "if only's" enter your mind?

_____

_____

_____

_____

For each "if only" write a realistic statement to balance it.

_____

_____

_____

_____

_____

_____

With the first news of loss, our mind acts as a filter. It immediately sifts through the facts and details, offering only the barest to keep us informed. Too much detail would be more than we could bear. So our mind filters and filters until our bodies and hearts can cope with a little more. At some point, when the body has recovered somewhat, the mind lets larger blocks of information in. At this point, by human instinct, we look for resolution. We struggle to make sense of what has happened and that is where the instant replay begins. We explore every option—even the outlandish. These explorations are what allow us to slowly internalize the fact that life, as we once knew it, has changed.

This is a pivotal point in the grieving process. At this point, or close to it, we are finally acknowledging the death in reality.

The "if only" Mind Game

"If only" is the game of guilt that plagues many survivors. The "if only" questions surface intensely in cases of unexpected death. The situation is so "out of control" that our human nature fights and searches for a way to control the uncontrollable. As we yearn to make sense of the senseless, often the only route of control we find is to blame ourselves.

"I should have known," or "If only I had talked to him for two minutes longer..." are sentiments that those who grieve may say to themselves. Realize this guilt is a way of trying to gain control over the uncontrollable and then work to let it go. Each time it enters, remember that this is our longing for control, but don't give in to the guilt. You cannot change what has happened and odds are you couldn't have changed it beforehand. No one knows these things are going to happen—no one has that much control.

Anger

Who wouldn't be angry when someone they loved so dearly is suddenly taken from them? Anger is a natural part of the grieving process. Yet anger takes different forms, some of them healthy and some of them unhealthy.

Let's examine the types of anger that are natural, though unhealthy. Some of us will express anger when we are not getting the support we need from friends, family or work. While intensely wrapped in our grief, we usually don't think to ask for support. Instead we lash out at those close to us with hostility, irritability and anger. If we can recognize this anger for what it is, we can use it in a healthy way. This can be our cue that we are not receiving the support that we need. We need to ask for more or seek out other support networks.

Displaced anger is simply misdirected anger. We want someone to take responsibility for what has happened. We need someone to blame and to be held accountable. We may scream or yell at those who cared for the person at the hospital. We may become angry with those who were with the person when he died. Displaced anger is completely natural and will lessen as you learn to accept what has happened.

Anger can also surface when we recall past moments or turmoil, pain or unresolved issues within our relationship with the person we have lost. Suddenly we are forced to realize we will never share another physical interaction with this person. When that happens, memories flood through. Within these memories there are bound to be recollections of feisty exchanges, arguments and past hurts.

Wishing we had more time with the loved one, we may over-criticize ourselves for any time there was conflict in the past. It is unrealistic, however, to expect perfection in any relationship. Immersing ourselves in the "should haves" and "could haves" of the past will only prevent us from dealing effectively with our anger in the present.

What "should haves" and "could haves" do you recite to yourself?

_____

_____

_____

_____

_____

_____

_____

Take a moment and feel each of your "should haves" and "could haves" intensely. Then let them go. Realize the past is the past. What anger surfaces? Write about it below.

_____

_____

_____

_____

_____

_____

_____

Anger also occurs when we suppress our feelings. Anger is not the most accepted emotion in today's culture. In fact, many people don't even recognize anger as part of the grieving process. Depending on our support network and situation we may be encouraged not to show our anger. When this happens, the anger still exists and needs to be released, so it is released inward. This can cause a variety of problems. We may become sick, depressed, have chronic pain or begin having nightmares.

Below, list healthy alternatives for releasing anger.

_____

_____

_____

_____

Anger is especially common with tragic deaths. Since we could do nothing to stop or prevent the loss, and are left only to interpret it, we may become frustrated and develop feelings of helplessness. Bouts of crying are the most common release for this anger. It's easy to not release this anger and to turn it inward. If you suspect you may be doing so, talk to a friend or counselor to help release these feelings.

As you look at your grieving process, do you feel you have expressed your anger? If so, how? (Write about it below.) If you are having problems identifying your anger, you likely have not faced it yet.

_____

_____

_____

_____

Appropriate anger is the point that we all hope to get to eventually. In this phase we can take our anger, in whatever form, and vent it. There are many ways to release anger appropriately. Here are a few... place a checkmark next to any that you think would be helpful to you. Try one of these exercises the next time you find yourself upset.

- ☐ beat a pillow
- ☐ create a sacred space where you can go and not be heard or seen to let the anger out of your system
- ☐ use journaling to record and release your angry feelings
- ☐ take a walk out into an unpopulated area and scream until you are exhausted
- ☐ talk with a friend, therapist or counselor
- ☐ have a good cry, let the tears flow

Screaming Exercise

Sometimes the only thing left to do is SCREAM! Emotions may well up inside you and they need a place to go. It can be both a release and a relief to scream as loud as you can and to say whatever comes to mind. It will be a challenge to find an appropriate place to do this exercise. You may have to travel some distance to find a wide open space where no one can hear you. Here is an example of how Pam and her sister Marilyn solved the problem:

"A few months after my sister's husband died suddenly and I was still reeling from George's death, we decided to go to Canada to attend a workshop. In our free time we drove across vast empty spaces with miles of road and no one around. We found ourselves in the car one afternoon in the middle of a Canadian "no man's land" highway screaming 'Why did you die!,' 'I hate you for dying!' 'This death stuff really sucks!' and a host of other expletives. We laughed at how ridiculous we sounded and we cried because we needed to. We decided it was safest if the one who wasn't crying drove the car because it's hard to see the road with tears in your eyes! "

Our intense emotions need to have an outlet, otherwise they can make us sick. A very potent outlet for our grief is to find a private location (your parked car can serve this purpose very well) and SCREAM and RANT as loudly as you can. By giving ourselves permission to do this, we validate ourselves and our healing process. Do not stifle this need to give voice to your pain. It is your right as a human being to express your deepest feelings in this way if you choose to do so.

Record your feelings after completing this exercise.

_____

_____

_____

_____

_____

_____

_____

_____

_____

_____

_____

_____

Fear

Throughout our grief work, fear can be debilitating. Some people experience fear in a small number of areas, while others are overwhelmed by it. It is perfectly natural to be fearful. We have experienced the most unexpected tragedy. Common fears include: fearing any situation that remotely resembles how the loved one died, fearing that others we love will be harmed, fearing we will be unable to go on, fearing we will die ourselves and fearing the simplest activities will lead to tra gedy.

Fear serves several purposes. In the initial stages of grief it gives us something to focus on besides the death that has taken place. It also offers potential control. If we fear that riding in a car could kill us, and choose not to ride in a car, we create the illusion of control. As explained earlier, with tragic death it's common to seek any control we can find. Most of the time, fear will run its course naturally. The worksheet below can help you work through your fears. If you find your fears become dehabilitating, seek the help of a professional.

What do you fear?

_____

_____

_____

_____

Is this fear rational or irrational? _____

Most of our fears are irrational and by writing out the irrationality we equi p ourselves with the strength to fight our fear. How, Specifically , is your fear irrational?

_____

_____

_____

_____

The next time your fear surfaces, refer back to what you wrote above. If a new fear occurs in this fear's place, repeat the process.

Depression, or Is It Appropriate Sadness?

Do not confuse depression with sadness. If you are crying a lot because you have lost someone through tragic and sudden death, you are sad, not depressed. If you find yourself immobilized, unable to concentrate, sleeping too much or too little, you are grieving, you are not depressed. Some other characteristics of this stage are:

- weakness and feeling drained
- loss of appetite
- extreme fatigue
- extreme irritability
- unresponsiveness
- inability to focus or concentrate
- feeling hopeless or powerless
- aches and pains
- lack of personal hygiene
- a feeling that the world is not a safe place

In her book *The Courage to Grieve*, Judy Tatelbaum writes, "So much of our energy is tied up inside that little energy is available for the action of functioning. We may be moody. At times we may feel pain and weep, and then at other times we may feel detached and without emotion. During this period we may be withdrawn and unable to relate to other people. Negativity, pessimism, emptiness and a temporary sense of meaninglessness of life are all symptoms of depression. 'What's the use?' or 'Why bother?' are typical feelings. We may be acutely restless and then become immobile. The essential thing to remember is that the pain of grief is never constant and does not last forever. Throughout this middle phase of mourning, the myriad of feelings of grief come and go in waves, with lessening intensity as time goes on."

Again, if you feel stuck in this stage, you may need professional intervention. For most, however this stage can be described as situational depression, meaning it should subside after a time.

Are you suffering from any of the above symptoms? If so, for how long? If these symptoms persist for more than 6 weeks or become troubling, seek professional help.

_____

_____

_____

_____

_____

_____

Calming Exercises

Stress, anxiety, sadness, depression—these emotions can leave us knotted inside. Practicing deep breathing exercises can help us to relax and unwind our wound-up-emotions. The following exercises will help calm you during trying times.

Place one hand on your abdomen. As you inhale, you want to feel the movement in your abdomen, not in your chest. Inhale for the count of ten, then exhale for the count of ten. Repeat this ten to fifteen times for deeper relaxation.

To relax your whole body, lay down in a quiet place. Breathe deeply, slowly inhaling and exhaling. Beginning with your left leg, clench your muscles as tightly as you can for the count of three. Then relax them. Do the same with the right leg, left arm and right arm. Then move up your body tightening your pelvis, then stomach, then chest, then shoulders, then neck and lastly facial muscles. When you have completed this exercise you should feel extremely calm and peaceful. Visualize an ocean beach or other calming scene to deepen the relaxed feelings.

If you like, record your visualization experience in the space below.

_____

_____

_____

_____

_____

_____

_____

_____

_____

_____

Multiple Grief

Some people have multiple situations they are dealing with on top of their grief. Perhaps an elderly parent is ill, you are sending a child off to college, you are going through menopause, or a career change, or completing college or some other challenging life situation. These multiple situations can halt, delay or complicate the primary grieving process. When we have many stressful experiences, much of our emotional energy is funneled into these stressors. We are left with little reserve. Yet, in order to heal we must find a way to cope with these stressors, while still feeling and exploring our grief.

Although one experience may stand out in your mind, any other losses are likely to be important as well. Even things that might seem small or insignificant, in the face of tragedy, can complicate the grieving process when they accumulate. Soon we find ourselves stuck in a web of turmoil, unable to unravel our complicated feelings. Many events have mixed together and we can't pull on a single string to undue the knot—instead a tug on a single string just makes the knot tighter.

To work through Multiple Grief, it's important to recognize each of the components that you are grieving. Once you have identified those components you can begin to focus on healing. Take your time in identifying these components—they may not come to the surface at first! If you find that you are still facing acute grief after a long period, you may want to come back to this exercise. Sometimes we suppress other losses that get caught up in the web. For example, a loss you are facing now might remind you of the abense of a parent during a difficult period in your life. Although this may not have been a death, it is a loss, and losses (not only deaths) are what lead to the experience of Multiple Grief.

What is the most recent experience you are grieving?

_____

_____

_____

_____

Are there any other experiences in the past 5 years that you grieved or are greiving over?

_____

_____

_____

_____

_____

_____

_____

_____

_____

_____

For each of the experiences you listed, did you move through the different stages of grieving, or did you stop somewhere in the process without ever fully coming to terms with your grief? If you stopped, mid-process, where did you stop?

_____

_____

_____

_____

Are there any other times of loss that your current experience resurrects in your mind?

_____

_____

_____

When you have listed all of your grief you will know, because you will feel both a sadness and a relief inside. Until that point, you will feel a gnawing ache, as if you are trying to excavate a very embedded rock. You do not need to remember, recall or record everything at once. Do not force it. Simply continue returning to this exercise, excavating a bit more each time.

Grief Sessions

Once you have listed-out those things which you need to grieve in your life, you may find it helpful to schedule "Grief Sessions". Grief Sessions are set times where you honor your feelings. In our busy days we tend to immerse ourselves in "things" and "work" so we don't experience our grief. But we can't get through what we do not feel.

Brook found it helpful to create a private space to grieve. Always the "strong one" in the family, she was unable to "break down" and grieve fully while in her own house, or within her roles as mother, wife and worker. She found that taking a day or a weekend away to change her enviornment, even if it was a cheap hotel, allowed her the space to let out and face her emotions.

Other people find success in spending an hour taking a walk and getting in touch with their grief. Some people can sit outside with a journal and express their feelings. Just as our grief is unique, so will our "Grief Sessions" be.

Write down some ideas for your own Grief Sessions—then schedule one on your calendar.

_____

_____

_____

_____

_____

_____

My first Grief Session will be on (list date/place)

_____

_____

_____

Coping with Guilt

If you are suffering from the "if onlys" or the "I should haves," and you are left with a deep feeling of regret that you couldn't have done more to help your loved one or prevent the death, try the following exercise:

Below, write at least a one page letter to the individual who died. Tell them whatever you want but remember to include the following:

- the facts of what happened
- how you feel about what happened
- how their death has affected your life

Now, turn the page over and imagine the deceased responding to your letter. Asking questions of the deceased will make this exercise extremely valuable. So write down such questions as, "How do you feel about what happened?" and "Will you please forgive me for _____?" "Have I been punished enough for my part (real or imagined) in all of this and is there anything else I can do to show you how sorry I am?" "How can I show you how much I have suffered?" Then close your eyes and answer each question as if they were speaking through you.

If you find this is a difficult exercise to do on your own you may want to ask a therapist or trusted friend to sit quietly with you. **Caution:** If you are being "told" by your inner voice to hurt yourself in any way, seek professional help immediately.

Use the space below and on the following page to write a letter to your loved one.

_____

_____

_____

_____

_____

_____

_____

Now write back to yourself, imagining how your loved one would respond.

Self-Check

As you work through your grief, it's important to monitor yourself and your stages. The following list can help you discern healthy grief from distorted grief. If you feel you may be suffering unhealthy grief, seek the help of a support group, clergy person or therapist.

Check any stages you are experiencing.

- ☐ **Extreme Avoidant Behavior** – If you are avoiding friends and family for a prolonged period of time (over three weeks) you will want to talk to a professional. People need other people to work through grief.

- ☐ **Lack of Self-Care** – In order to have the energy and emotional capacity to work through grief, one must first take care of his/her basic needs. If you are having problems meeting basic needs, this is a warning sign to seek help. (A 24 to 72-hour bout of decreased self-care is normal. If you cannot take care of your most basic needs—food, sleep, showering, etc.—seek outside assistance.)

- ☐ **Prolonged Denial** – If months have passed and you are still in denial, you will most likely need a support group to help you move through this stage.

- ☐ **Self-Destructive Thoughts** – These thoughts are not unusual during grief but we can expect them to pass quickly. If they are persistent or obsessive it is best to consult a professional for guidance in working through them. If any of these thoughts involve serious harm to yourself (or someone else) seek help immediately.

- ☐ **Displaced Anger** – With few emotional outlets available to us, it is common for anger to be displaced. However, this can become problematic if your anger is hurting you in personal or professional areas, or hurting others—seek help immediately.

- ☐ **Prolonged Depression or Anxiety** – Like denial, prolonged and immobilizing depression or anxiety are signs to seek professional help.

- ☐ **Self-Medication** – If you are using substances in excess to self-medicate your pain, i.e. food, alcohol or drugs, seek the help of an organization that specializes in such disorders or the help of a professional.

- ☐ **Revenge or Retribution** – If you are preoccupied with revenge or retribution toward someone affiliated with your loss, seek immediate help. This is a very dangerous deversion that cannot be taken lightly.

Chapter Four
Making Sense of the World Around You

"The doorbell rang at around eight-thirty. I wasn't expecting anyone, so a strange feeling came over my heart. I peeked out the keyhole, and saw my brother, Denver, and sister-in-law, Allison, standing in the hallway. I let them in. There was a deep silence, and I knew from my brother's eyes what had happened. He didn't even have to speak. He took me in his arms, and my world changed forever. My eyes moved to a picture of my son as a child, his red hair cropped close to his head, and his big blue eyes looking out at me. My world was turning to darkness, and I would never live in it the same again." —Singer Judy Collins on the death of her son, Clark

When we grapple with sudden loss, we are forced to reconsider some assumptions about ourselves. We may begin to feel vulnerable and sense that life is tenuous. We may begin to question whether or not the world is meaningful and orderly. We may see ourselves as weak and needy for the first time. Those who haven't had to deal with the trauma of a sudden death may also come to question these assumptions; but they are not forced to question the basic truth of these assumptions in the same way a survivor must.

We are all forced to confront our mortality. Most people deal with this issue in mid-life. It is then that we begin to see signs of our own aging, or we face the imminent death of our parents or grandparents. This is the natural order of things. However, as survivors of sudden death we are forced to confront our mortality at the time of the trauma—regardless of our age. A heightened sense of the fundamental fragility of life quickly emerges —usually within minutes, hours or days of the death.

Aphrodite Matsakis, Ph.D. says in her book, *Trust After Trauma*, "…although it can empower them to try to make the most out of life, it can also be frightening and overwhelming not only to themselves, but also to others who, quite understandably, prefer to avoid confronting the inevitability of their own deaths."

You may have thought, "It can't happen to me." But it did happen and you may no longer feel the world is a safe place. Feelings of vulnerability can bring on a sense of doom or an expectation that your own future may be foreshortened. You may also experience an intense fear that the trauma may repeat itself and another family member, lover or friend will die.

Dr. Matsakis goes on to say, "The just world philosophy cannot explain what happened to you. You used to think that if you were careful, honest, and good, you could avoid disaster. But the trauma taught you that all of your best efforts could not prevent the worst from happening. Perhaps you saw others who were also innocent die or be unfairly injured. So, while you would like to believe that the world is orderly, and that good is rewarded and evil is punished, you had an experience that contradicts these beliefs."

When our foundation is swept from beneath us, we begin questioning the fundamentals of life. As crazy as it seems, this shattering of assumptions is necessary in grief. We must re-evaluate what we once held as true, move through the ruin, and create a new foundation based on what we have learned.

What beliefs are you questioning? Remember, it's okay to question anything and everything. Be true to yourself in your answer.

_____

_____

_____

_____

_____

_____

_____

_____

_____

_____

_____

_____

_____

_____

_____

_____

Loss of Purpose

Many grievers feel a loss of purpose. After all, we've known a life that has been certain. We were certain that a person would be there, we never questioned. Suddenly, all we have left are questions—questions like: Why did this happen? If a person can die so suddenly—what is the purpose of trying for accomplishment and trying to live? Brook battled this concept in the wake of her brother, Caleb's death.

"I have always been an over-achiever. I scheduled and organized my life so I could climb mountain after mountain in search of reaching some higher place. When Caleb died, I wondered what the purpose of all the climbing was. I suddenly realized there was no guarantee I would live to be seventy—or even another week. So what was the purpose of all this sowing—if the chance to reap could be taken away?

Lost inside this question, I turned to a wonderful friend and my local pastor, Jeff. We often had lunch together and I always found comfort in his words. I stared at him across the table, and said simply— 'What does anything matter?' He responded with a sentence, which was a riddle in itself. He simply said, 'Because nothing matters, everything matters.' I tried over lunch to comprehend the sentence as it twirled through my mind. Finally, I asked him to interpret further.

Jeff explained that looking long term or planning ahead cannot matter. Sure we need to be somewhat prepared for the future, but to become overly preoccupied is foolish since life can disappear so quickly. 'Everything you do at this very instant is what matters,' he explained. 'You should be living life, right now. Anyone who lives for tomorrow is a fool.' At the time, I had been juggling a few thoughts on where to go with my writing career and what project to pursue next. The thought of having a whole book in front of me seemed daunting and purposeless. I was scared to start something, scared perhaps that I would never finish it. Jeff asked me what mattered most at that very moment. "Getting by," was my reply. As our eyes met, I knew that was what mattered. I would write about getting by because that meant something to me, and if life went away tomorrow, I would be content in where I was today."

Since nothing of the future matters, everything in the here and now does. To learn to live in the present, to reap the gifts of the moment, is the best tribute we can give to anyone, much less ourselves.

How can you live "more in the moment" and less in the past and future?

_____

_____

_____

_____

_____

When Faith is Shattered

If our spiritual faith has been shattered, perhaps all we can expect from the grieving process is some form of transcendence. Gail Sheehy describes this beautifully in her seminal work entitled, *Pathfinders*, where she writes, "Transcendence is a realm beyond all the negative emotions of mourning, beyond even the neutral point of acceptance. When it happens that a life accident creates a 'pathfinder', the person is able to transcend his former self as well. A positive self-fulfilling prophecy is made as one comes out of the dark hours. And around a new work, idea, purpose, faith, or a love inspired by the accident, one's goals are realigned. Transcendence is an act of creativity. One creates a partial replacement for what has been lost. The light at the end of mourning is glimpsed, and it is cause for new joy."

It's common to question God in these dark times. We may lose faith in God, a faith we thought would never change or waiver. In *The Grief Recovery Handbook*, John W. James and Russell Freidman write, "We have to be allowed to tell someone that we're angry at God and not be judged for it, or told that we're bad because of it. If not, this anger may persist forever and block spiritual growth. We've known people who never returned to their religion because they weren't allowed to express their true feelings. If this happens, the griever is cut off from one of the most powerful sources of support he or she might have."

For most of us, this loss of faith is temporary and if we ask our clergy person or faith community, they should willingly help us with this struggle. It is common for grievers to yell, scream at God or lose faith. One should not feel guilty for such emotions. Like many other aspects of grief, this is part of our need as we work through the process. Even Pam's faith was tested during her experience with sudden loss...

"I remember walking up and down the halls of the hospital where George lay on life support, shaking my fist at Heaven, yelling at God. Someone who overheard suggested that I not be angry with God and that I control how I speak to Him. I replied, 'My God can handle this anger. And I know if I get angry at God, God won't desert me.'"

The anonymous poem found on the following page can be comforting to recite when we are feeling lost and our faith is being tried.

Prayer of Faith

We trust that beyond absence
There is a presence.

That beyond the pain
there can be healing.

That beyond the brokenness
there can be wholeness.

That beyond the anger
there may be peace.

That beyond the hurting
there may be forgiveness.

That beyond the silence
there may be the Word.

That beyond the Word
there may be understanding.

That through understanding
there is love.

- author unknown

Writing A Prayer

Try writing a prayer sharing your feelings with God. Let Him know about your fears, your sadness, your doubts, your insecurities. The first step in healing any relationship is to relay how we feel. The same is true of your relationship with God. You may choose to keep an ongoing prayer journal.

_____

_____

_____

_____

_____

_____

_____

_____

_____

_____

_____

_____

_____

Learning through Loss

Patricia lost her fourteen-year-old son, Doug, to a self-inflicted gunshot wound. She offers ten affirmations of life that she learned from her grieving process:

1. **"I let my feelings flow**; they are my life's blood; they will not kill me; they will heal me.

   (By the way, a punching bag is a good way to move from rage to tears.)

2. **I follow my lead.** I only need to know and then honor the next step.

3. **I can trust the Universe** to support me and it will in ways seen and unseen.

4. **Help is there—**I need only let it in at times, to ask others and to trust that people want

   to help in these ways:

   Physically—mow my lawn, scrub my deck (where my son died)

   Metaphysically—pray for me, hold me in the light

   Psychologically—send me your memories of Doug, poems that mean something to you

5. **I will confront my demons.** Anxieties are not stoppers or signs to give up, they are just a new place to step slowly and to be creative.

6. **Gratitude**—every situation has a gift and a limit. I won't deny the limits and the pain and I will let myself see the gifts and the goodness as well.

7. **Be there as a friend**—the greatest gift I can give to someone is to accept him or her fully as they are.

8. **Life is a journey**, not a destination. I will live each day fully for its gifts of grief and gladness.

9. **Grief comes in waves.** Each carries me forward to the next step. An ocean never becomes stagnant water.

10. **I will pray**, meditate and stay in touch with the spirit in whatever way works for me. "

Patricia's final note: "Upon completion of this... a fresh wave of grief hit as spring and Easter arrived. I found myself needing to read what I had written over and over to remember the lessons I had so painfully learned. Which brings me to an old affirmation of mine...I will tell a friend what I see as my truth so that someday when I forget, my friend can tell it back to me. So dear reader, help me remember when times get tough."

Patricia chose to use the power of lessons learned in facing her grief. This practice is both healing and empowering. Try it for yourself. Purchase a small and beautifully bound book at a stationary store. In this book, record the lessons you learn moving through the grief process. It can be a great reminder of the steps you are taking and a wonderful way to become more aware of purpose and meaning. – *Contributed by Patricia Ellen*

On the following page, list lessons you have learned from your grief.

What I've Learned Along the Way

(see previous page for instructions)

What My Loved One Has Left Me

When someone dies suddenly, it is not unusual to have a sense that one was rejected or abandoned in some way. When you are feeling the searing pain and anger of abandonment, it is even more difficult to consider that your pain may be transformed into something meaningful or that the end of the relationship through death can be in any way beneficial to your growth. It can be. Especially if you were dependent on the other person for good feelings about yourself. Now is the time to look within and to affirm yourself as a person of value. It is also the time to remember and replay the positive messages you received from your significant other before they died. Everyone has heard at least one life affirming, positive message or compliment from their deceased loved one, worth repeating to oneself.

Record positive messages you received from your loved one in the space provided below. You may even want to photocopy this sheet and carry it with you for a time. Allow these positive messages to lift and inspire you.

_____

_____

_____

_____

_____

_____

_____

_____

_____

_____

Redefining Ourselves

When we lose someone, we often lose a piece of ourselves. The closer our relationship with the person, the more of our self we have to redefine. Much of our identity comes from our relationship to others. Take the woman who has called herself a wife and mother for 30 years and then loses her family in a plane crash. This woman whose identity was wife and mother, is left without a husband or children. Defining ourselves by others can bring fullness to our lives, but when faced with loss it also means we must redefine the resulting emptiness.

One of the first things to remember as you seek your own redefinition is that you don't need to know all the answers now. No one will force you or hold "a clock to your head" asking you to redefine yourself over night. Redefinition is a process. It involves soul-searching, courage and rediscovery. It takes time. Realize that you don't have to let go of who you were—you just need to adapt for the future. In the case above, the mentioned woman will always know what it was like to be a wife and a mother. For the rest of her life, she will act as a wife and mother in her thoughts and actions because that is what she was for 30 years. Even though life turns itself upside down and our role may change suddenly, we can't deny the way we have lived in the past.

Simply stated, the question becomes, "Now what?" After expecting life to take a certain course, it has chosen it's own, far from your plans. Again, take it slow. Choose one thing that you know for certain. If you have always loved to paint, know that in the future you can still be a painter. Focus on what you do know about yourself. Look at the things you've always wanted to try and pick one to focus on. Take it one step at a time, and as you're ready, add another "piece" to yourself.

What are the things you know for certain?

_____

_____

_____

_____

_____

_____

_____

For some this rebuilding takes months, for others it can take a lifetime, but piece-by-piece you can rebuild. When you are ready to begin the rebuilding process, try the exercises on the following pages. They will be waiting for you when you are ready.

Thank You Exercise

As you continue to grow and heal you will eventually discover at least something (no matter how seemingly insignificant) for which you can express gratitude. If the expression is not available to you now, it is probably a temporary condition.

After you have honored your anger, and when you are ready, you might want to try this Thank You Exercise. Compared to all other acts, personal and spiritual growth is greatest through the expression of gratitude. No matter how difficult at first, expressing appreciation for the life that is gone can help make some meaning in the face of the tragedy. Acknowledging, in writing, what was empowering and uplifting about your relationship to the deceased, will help you keep sacred what you had together—to retain what was valuable and to let go of the false belief that they are incapable of inspiring you (now that they are dead).

Why pick up a pen and write a note... why not? The act of writing, choosing the type of pen and paper, the color of the ink, moving the pen across the paper, seeing the words—all make what you are saying more real—more concrete. You will notice your energy shift—from confusion about what to write; from anger at having to sort through your life for the first time (or the thousandth time); from your tears as you recognize what you have lost; and ultimately, to a sense of relief at having given yourself the chance to express the unsaid.

Date and save your notes in a special place or put them in your journal. Eventually, you may want to destroy the note. Remember, this is about expressing feelings that need to be expressed. Rereading it again, however, after several months or years is sometimes useful, so you may want to save it for future reference. It is also useful to write another note after some time has passed. Each time you write, you will gain new insights. If you have young children you may even want to read your notes to them when they are older.

You will find an example on the following page.

Dear Jim,

Thanks for the holding. You were good at holding when I needed to be held—when I was having trouble learning to trust—you helped me to know that I was capable of loving.

You held me when I was sad. I had so much sadness then. Thank you for the many times you were able to say, "Everything will be all right." Thank you for coming into this lifetime. This time I received the lesson I was so long denying that I needed to learn. What did I learn? I learned that it is unwise to marry someone to give you what you didn't get from your parents as a child. It is important to nurture and love yourself.

Thank you for being a good father to our son—you were the kind of father I would have wanted for myself. Thank you for the 10 years of our marriage—for 10 years I felt loved. Thanks for being with me at the birth of our son and for supporting us so I could stay home with him when he was a baby—yes, MOST OF ALL, thank you for our son for without you, he would not have been born .....

Love, Joan

Although the author of this letter sobbed on and off for the better part of an hour after writing this, she admitted to experiencing a sense of relief and to feeling better about herself than she had in some time. She affirmed why she had chosen the man she did and felt great comfort in this.

Use the space on the following page to write your own Thank You Letter when you are ready.

Thank You Letter

Seeking Meaning

(to be done 1-2 years after the loss)

How can one expect to make meaning of a suddenly ended life, an aborted relationship, a disrupted lifestyle and the painful losses that go along with it? These are profound questions, which are not easily addressed. There are no flip responses or boilerplate answers. However, what can be offered as a pathway to healing, are possibilities and new perspectives you may not have investigated. You are welcome to "try on" these possibilities, knowing they will either fit your understanding and give you some peace of mind and stillness of heart, or conversely create even more questions for you. In any case, the exploration into why your relationship with the deceased needed to begin and to end may well be worth the energy invested.

It is best to answer these questions when you have uninterrupted time. Make sure you are calm and relaxed. Play some soft music. You may want to open your exploration with a short prayer.

Explore and freewrite answers to the following questions:

Could the relationship have ended just when a particular phase of change and growth was completed for you? Could it be that you are now being catapulted into a greater phase of growth—that in spite of your tremendous loss and disrupted life, that a new you, full of vital life force and creativity is ready to emerge (or has already emerged)?

_____

_____

_____

_____

_____

_____

_____

_____

_____

Look at your life in totality to this point. Think about your life before you met the deceased. Think about your life with this person when they were alive. What lessons did you learn?

_____

_____

_____

_____

_____

_____

_____

What cycle was occurring? For what purpose do you think this person was "sent" into your life?

_____

_____

_____

_____

_____

_____

_____

_____

_____

We believe that every opportunity, no matter how painful, offers growth if we are strong enough to meet the challenge. What life lesson could this person have taught you? What growth might their time in your life have encouraged? What might their death encourage?

_____

_____

_____

_____

_____

_____

_____

_____

What characteristics could this experience unveil within you?

_____

_____

_____

_____

These are tough questions and there is no need to answer them right away. In fact, this exercise is best a year or so down the road when you've had a bit more time to assimilate and reflect. When you are ready, though, we believe you will find the exploration valuable. Spend some time with these questions. Write about them in your journal. See what surfaces—and how what surfaces—might be the beginning of a new phase of life for you.

Defining Priorities

After losing a loved one the world often seems to have spun out of control and we are left trying to make sense of our place within it. Thinking about what is important to you and exploring ways you can make a difference can be very helpful. The following exercise asks you to identify your priorities. Keep in mind that there aren't any right or wrong answers.

What three things matter most to you?

_____

_____

_____

_____

What do you value most spiritually?

_____

_____

_____

_____

What do you value most emotionally?

_____

_____

_____

_____

What possessions do you value most?

_____

_____

_____

_____

What people are most important to you? (List them by name.)

_____

_____

_____

_____

What do you feel you need to accomplish to make your life worthwhile?

_____

_____

_____

_____

When you die, how would you like to be remembered?

_____

_____

_____

_____

What are two things you could do each and every day, to make every day special?

_____

_____

_____

_____

What in your life are you most grateful for?

_____

_____

_____

_____

After answering the previous questions, record what you discovered about yourself. Answer these questions in your entry:

1. What are the most important elements of life for me? (Often you'll discover a common thread in your answers.)
2. Based on what I've learned, how would I describe a fulfilling life for myself?
3. What steps can I take now to move toward that fulfilling life? What steps can I take later?

Finding a Beginning, Middle and End

Questions abound, when we lose someone tragically. Unlike those who lose someone through a terminal illness, we have little or no time to question doctors, understand a diagnosis, struggle with our faith or say our goodbyes.

Yet through our upbringing we learn to understand life in terms of cycles. We understand the cycle of age. We know the cycle of schooling. We know the cycle of work. We know the cycles of diet and exercise. Almost everything can be understood as a cycle with a beginning, middle and end. Our minds will immediately try to do the same with our tragic loss experience. Our mind will look for the beginning (What happened?), the middle (How did he/she feel, respond, progress?), the end (Was he in pain? Did he have any last thoughts or words?) Yet unless we were present, we are left with question after question. In order to get to a place where we can think about the experience in its entirety, we must know as much of the cycle as possible.

This is why it is so natural to talk with others about our loved one's last moments. Over and over again, grievers tell their stories, attempting to make sense of them, attempting to understand the cycle. Often, there are ways to get more information. Police, witnesses and doctors can all offer clues to what happened. When we have enough clues we can piece together a story that will allow our questioning to lessen. As our questions lessen, we create more room to heal.

Dr. Ann Kaiser Stearns, author of *Coming Back: Rebuilding Lives After Crisis and Loss* offers the following suggestion: "Make a conscious effort to identify what is not making sense to you about your loss or crisis. You might ask yourself: What is it about the situation and/or about his or her death that is most puzzling or troubling to me? What part of grief is troubling me? What other things are troubling me?"

Before seeking your own beginning, middle and end, this can be a useful exercise. Confront your questions. Explore your feelings and record these thoughts. Use this as a guideline to gather the information you will need.

Brook found that she and her mother had many questions:

"For starters, my mother and I had never heard of the term anaphylactic shock—we couldn't even pronounce it. Our initial disbelief was so strong, not a single question was asked at the hospital. But as the days went by, the questions came one after the other. Caleb had been stung a month before—was this a cumulative effect of venom? Several years prior he had had chest pains that went undiagnosed—could his death be connected to that? Had any blood been drawn and a firm allergic reaction determined? If his death certificate said 12:54 and his friends said he was unconscious at 11:15 —what happened between then and 12:54?

I did as much research as I could and then I called the doctor. I immediately put him at rest by letting him know that I trusted he had done everything in his capacity, and I did not, in any way, question his ability. I let the doctor know that my questions were more about figuring out the order of events. We talked for close to an hour.

After combining his comments with my research, I was able to confidently assume that Caleb did die from a fatal reaction to a bee sting. He was dead before the ambulance arrived, or minutes after, and unconscious long before that. He was not pronounced dead until 12:54

because the doctors were praying for a miracle. Being so young and healthy, they worked extensively on him in the E.R. trying anything they could to revive him.

I also was able to learn that bee allergies are typically not hereditary. However, I also learned, those who know they are allergic can carry an Epinephrine shot, that can possibly reverse the reaction, allowing more time to get to medical treatment.

With this knowledge and for my own peace of mind, I went to a specialist in the allergy field. I asked the allergist to test both my three-year-old daughter and myself. He took our blood and sent it to the Mayo clinic for analysis. The tests came back negative. Yet, since this allergy can develop at any time, he gave us both adrenaline kits so that we would feel more at ease. While only 40 to 60 people a year die from fatal reactions to insects, it was important for me to have that comfort. "

Talking to others will help you get the information you need to find your own beginning, middle and end. This information-gathering can be a major catalyst in moving past the grief of "what happened?" to the process of rebuilding. It allows the mind to cycle through the event in its entirety, instead of stopping to question and getting lost in the who, what, when, where, why and how.

What do you know for certain about the death of your loved one?

_____

_____

_____

_____

_____

What questions do you have?

_____

_____

_____

_____

Can you research the answers to those questions, or contact someone to help you find the answers?

_____

_____

_____

_____

_____

When will you contact that person or do the research?

_____

_____

What information did you learn from your research?

_____

_____

_____

_____

_____

_____

_____

_____

Take a page or two to write the beginning, middle and end of *your* story.

Chapter Five
Grief Blocks

"It comes to all. We know not when,
or how, or why. It's always been
a mystery, a frightening thing,
enshrouded in the silencing.

When suddenly a loved one dies
we seem to sort of paralyze,
to just stop still within our track.
And oh, how much we want them back."

excerpted from *When A Loved One Dies,*
by Dolores Dahl, *Suddenly Alone*

Grieving is like a foreign land to most of us; a land where we find ourselves speaking and hearing an inner language we cannot comprehend. Because it can help to have a guide in our foreign land, this chapter will describe ways we commonly avoid grief and why we do so.

I Don't Want to Talk About It

You've got to talk about it, and talk about it, and talk about it some more. Find someone who will listen and talk until you can't talk anymore...at least for the moment. Then when you need to talk again, start all over with your story. Talking about it is an extremely important task, if you try to skip it, you will be blocked indefinitely. It is a task that will help you come to terms with the death and move you past the denial stage.

If you don't want to talk about it—try writing about it by answering the questions on the following pages. Answering these questions will not be a pleasant task and is not necessary if you are healthily talking through your experience with others. These questions are simply for those who are using avoidant behavior. Before we can heal, we must acknowledge. These questions serve as a step toward acknowledgement for those who are not talking with others.

Acknowledgement (see previous page to see if this is a page you need to complete)

The person I loved and lost was... _____

Describe briefly the circumstances of the death _____

_____

_____

_____

_____

_____

When I talk about my loss, I feel... _____

_____

_____

_____

_____

_____

_____

_____

I am scared that... _____

_____

_____

_____

Write down the name of a trusted friend, clergy person or professional with whom you could attempt to discuss your loss. _____

Help, I'm Stuck On Instant Replay

One of the horrors of instant replay is the persistent questioning of the choices we made. For example: Could I have called the ambulance sooner? If I'd known CPR would it have made a difference? Were there warning signs of the condition that I missed? Could I have done anything at all to prevent the tragedy? This kind of constant replay, over an extended period of time, blocks acceptance and closure.

Instant replay is the mind's way of coming to terms with the unfathomable. Some instant replay is necessary, but too much can keep us stuck. If your own instant replay is becoming an obsession, make an effort to do what therapists call "thought stopping." This is a technique whereby you consciously stop the thought, and deliberately change the subject. This is not a complicated task and is easier to do than you might think.

If the deceased's death was particularly troubling you may be replaying it over and over in your mind. If you have a horrible image of your loved one's last minutes or hours that runs over and over like a bad movie, first acknowledge the horror, then try shifting to an image of when you first met. Replace one image with the other.

Paul G. Stoltz, Ph.D., writes in his book entitled, *Adversity Quotient: Turning Obstacles into Opportunities*: "Arm yourself with 'STOPPERS'. Whenever a crisis strikes, anxiety is a frequent—and useless—response. It also spreads like an emotional wildfire making it impossible to apply rational steps to better cope with the problem. Soon you start to 'catastrophize' and feel helpless and hopeless. You squander energy and time worrying. To avoid imagining the worst will happen, use what I call 'stoppers' to regain control."

He continues, "When you feel overwhelmed, slap your knee or any hard surface. Shout, "Stop!" The sting will shock you into a more rational state. Some people leave a rubber band around their wrist. When they feel anxiety, they stretch it six inches and let it go.

Focus intently on an irrelevant object, such as a pen, the pattern of the wallpaper or a piece of furniture. If your mind is removed from the crisis, even for a moment, you can return with the calm you need to take effective action.

Take an activity break. Just 15 or 20 minutes of brisk walking or other exercise will clear your mind, raise your energy and flood your brain with endorphins—chemicals that put you in a more optimistic mood.

Put yourself in a setting where you're dwarfed by your surroundings. Catastrophizing makes problems larger than life. A shift in perspective will cut them down to size. Drive to the beach and look out over the ocean...stand at the base of a large tree...gaze up at the clouds...or listen to a great piece of music and let the grandeur wash over you."

What "STOPPER" can you try when you hit an instant replay? (You will also want to complete the Beginning, Middle and End exercise on page 56.)

_____

_____

Self-Judgment

Here is a sample of some internal, self-judging statements: "I'm not grieving right, I should be doing it differently. Perhaps I went back to work too soon. If I really loved him (or her), I'd be more devastated!"

This kind of self-judgment can block grief and is self-defeating at best. Perhaps you are looking at the way others grieve and are comparing yourself to them. Just as no two people are alike on this planet, no two people will "do grief" in exactly the same way. Some people will function at a very high level and some will not function at all. Some people will become introspective, others will cry, rant, scream and rage at the drop of a hat. These differences are largely influenced by the stage of grief you are in and your personality type. Cultural differences are also at play here, and men have a tendency to grieve differently than women. Another important variable, is the number of losses you have experienced in your life. Multiple losses compound and will influence how you handle your grief. (see page 30 for more on Multiple Grief.) We've said it many times, we all grieve in our own unique way. Stop the judgment and remove this block to healthy grief.

What unrealistic expectations do you have about the grieving process?

_____

_____

_____

Write a short note forgiving yourself for your hurtful self-talk; or write down the hurtful things you say on a separate piece of paper. Then rip it up and throw it out as a symbol of your release from self-judgement.

_____

_____

_____

_____

_____

_____

_____

I Feel so Guilty

In this case, you may be blocked by self-blame and you may be suffering from what is called, "survivor guilt". In *Survivor Guilt* author Aphrodite Matsakis, Ph.D. writes that; "Survivor guilt involves asking the existential question of why you suffer less than someone else, or why you lived while others died."

Of all the blocks mentioned in this chapter, guilt may be the strongest of all. Struggling with the question, "Why them, not me?" can create so much anxiety, pain and self-doubt that you stay stuck in your grief, much longer and more intensely than needed. You may feel that guilt is the way to "pay penance" for surviving, or that intense guilt is a way to honor your lost loved one. However, they want more for us, much more. Process your guilt with a trusted friend, therapist or clergy person. The best way to honor the deceased is to move through your guilt, put down the stick you use to beat yourself with and move on. (See the Guilt worksheet and exercise on page 33 for further assistance.)

You may also want to try and take a fresh perspective. What do you think your loved one would tell you about the guilt you are feeling? Write your thoughts below.

_____

_____

_____

_____

_____

_____

_____

_____

_____

_____

_____

Hurtful Self-Talk

Hurtful self-talk can block the grieving process—keeping you stuck. Sometimes it's easier to play "negative tapes" in our mind than to move through our pain toward healing. The healing process is tough—but there is a light at the end. Overcoming hurtful self-talk is an important step toward that light. The following statements are examples of commonly-felt hurtful self-talk that may run through our minds. Don't be ashamed if you identify with these statements. Place a check by each statement that you identify with, as a way to acknowledge it. Next, we will look at how to overcome these thoughts.

- My loved one is with God for a reason, so I shouldn't feel bad
- Grief is a mental illness
- It is wrong to feel anger at the deceased and it shouldn't be expressed
- If I acknowledge the loss, I'm afraid I will die too
- I should have died first
- If I allow my grief to surface, I'll go crazy
- If I grieve, people will think I'm weak
- If I appear sad too often, it will bring my family down
- If I cry in church, my fellow congregants will think I've lost faith
- If my children see me grieving, it will make them feel worse
- The deceased wouldn't want me to grieve
- Our life together was always happy—I don't want to remember the bad times
- I should have _____ (fill in the blank!)
- I should grin and bear it and put it behind me
- If I stop grieving people will expect me to be happy again.

When you find yourself running on the treadmill of hurtful self-talk it is important to come up with a positive statement for balance. Write down your destructive or hurtful thought and then write down a more positive, realistic thought. For example, "The deceased wouldn't want me to grieve," is hurtful. You could write, "The deceased would understand and respect the full spectrum of my emotions." Whenever a negative thought enters your mind, replace it with a positive, more realistic statement. Try "reprogramming" your hurtful self-talk below on the following page. Continue to add statements along with their positive counterparts as they occur to you throughout your journey.

66

Reprogramming Self-Talk

Hurtful Statement:

_____

_____

Positive Statement:

_____

_____

Hurtful Statement

_____

_____

Positive Statement

_____

_____

Hurtful Statement

_____

_____

Positive Statement

_____

_____

Chapter Six
Helping Children Cope with Grief

"In one of the stars
I shall be living
In one of them
I shall be laughing
And so it will be
As if all the stars
Were laughing
When you look
At the sky at night"
—The Little Prince
Antoine de Saint-Exipéry

As children grow, they will need to re-experience their loss at each stage of development. For example, at age five a child's understanding of death has moved from fantasy-based to reality-based. As they learn and understand more, they may need to review and re-experience the loss. When children realize the finality of death, they need to re-interpret what the death means to them. It's important to know this so that you don't feel you are "taking two steps backward," if your child becomes preoccupied with the loss at different stages of his/her develo pment.

One of the biggest challenges for children is the loss of their assumption that childhood is a safe place. Until that moment, young children believe they are immortal and invulnerable. Nothing could hurt their friends, parents or siblings. This deep trust is destroyed when they experience tragic loss at a young age.

A child's actions may change. It is not uncommon for a child to emotionally and physically regress during the grief process. The child may lash out, throw temper tantrums, do poorly in school, become shy or introverted, perform badly at once perfected skills, have nigh tmares and the like.

Patience and love are the keys to helping your child move past regression. This patience and love is only possible if you are doing your own grief work and renewing yourself emotionally.

Below you will find some common reactions children face while grieving:

Private Grieving
Children usually aren't as familiar or in tune with their emotions as adults. For this reason, many grieve privately. They may cry in their rooms or in the shower.

Unhealthy Anger

Children may choose unhealthy venues for releasing their anger. They may destroy things or engage in self-destructive behavior. It's important to remember that children do not have as many healthy outlets open to them as adults do. For this reason, it is imperative that we offer healthy outlets to teenagers.

Review page 23 on anger. Below, list several ways you, or another trusted adult, can help your child with this emotion.

_____

_____

_____

_____

Sexual Activity in Older Children

With the loneliness that accompanies grief, teenagers may be left feeling lonely and scared. They may feel family members don't have the energy or ability to comfort them since they are facing their own grief. For these reasons, it is not uncommon for teenagers to become sexually active in an attempt to ease the loneliness. If you are concerned that your child may become sexually active try talking to your child, or ask another trusted adult to broach the subject.

Guilty Feelings

From an early age children long to please their parents, family members and those close to them. Often they interpret an argument as their failure to please. Furthermore, they may feel responsible for the death because they didn't behave well, caused too many arguments, were a source of stress or didn't meet parents' expectations. While parents find this reasoning inconceivable, it can be common in a child's mind. It is very important to reiterate over and over again that the child or teenager was, in no way, responsible for the death. Older children may find the guilt exercise on page 33 helpful.

Physical Outbursts

Since children are less mature emotionally, they are much more likely to act out their emotions physically. This can take the form of tantrums, fighting, screaming, tattooing, body piercing or other physical expression. Watch for these physical signs. When you see one, realize it is probably caused by emotional repression. Take this as a red flag to find a support network or professional intervention for your child.

The Need to Be Away From Home in Older Children

When the deceased is a sibling, adolescents and teens may want to be away from the house. There are a couple of reasons for this. First, parents may be so absorbed in their own grief that children do not want to intensify their own emotions and grief by being around their parents. They may feel an obligation to comfort parents, yet not have the emotional energy to do so. Second, the house carries many memories of the relationship with their sibling and they may not be ready to face these memories. While it's important to maintain communication with the child and discuss their feelings, also offer the child his/her needed space, provided it's safe space.

Suicidal Thoughts

If the child was especially close to the person they have lost, they may see suicide as a way to rejoin their loved one. Also, when children are not dealing with their emotions in a healthy way they can quickly become overwhelmed. Suicide becomes an escape route from these turbulent emotions. When a child mentions or details any part of a suicidal plan, recognize this as an immediate sign to seek professional help.

Love and Support

During your child's grief, it is important to assure him or her of your love. Take a moment to write a letter to your child explaining your love for him, what you are proud of, how you sympathize and let your child know that you are there for him. Although he or she may not comment on your letter, behind closed doors it will be appreciated and re-read.

Outline the points you would like to cover in your letter in the space provided below.

_____

_____

_____

_____

_____

_____

_____

_____

_____

_____

General Guidelines for Helping Children

Below you will find some guidelines to review, as you work with understanding your children's experience and helping them through their grief.

- Children should not be discouraged from attending the funeral, memorial service or burial. Make sure you, or some other adult, holds their hand or sits close by to offer explanations and comfort.

- Children must be told that the person is dead. Do not say the deceased is on a "long trip" or in a "deep sleep". The child must be told that death is final and that there is no hope of the deceased returning. The child can then start to accept the finality of the situation and begin grieving.

- To help the child begin to mourn, a surviving parent needs to continue the daily routine as much as possible.

- Be supportive, understanding, open and accepting of their behavior.

- Work on listening. Communicating with a different generation can be difficult. Do your best to listen and be present without telling the child what to do. If you have a hard time listening objectively, find someone who can.

- Since a child's world has been turned upside down, it's important to remind them that you will always make sure their basic needs are taken care of.

- Continually express your unconditional love and acceptance.

- Answer questions as honestly as possible. Give as thorough answers as the child's age allows for.

- The child's environment should stay the same—this is not the time for a new school, a new house, or even a new baby-sitter.

- When you sense the child's readiness to grieve, it is okay to pray together, cry and reminisce together.

- Allow the child to talk, and talk, and talk about the death with you. Help him or her to understand that the grief will lessen and that the light will come again.

Remember, that no matter how old the child, they have experienced the worst possible tragedy. They will feel terrible. They should not be encouraged to forget or deny. They must learn, with your help and guidance, that they can overcome emotional catastrophes. Allowing the child to feel the full power of the sudden loss will help increase coping ability for the rest of the child's life.

Take a moment to think about your child. What information and support do they need from you? How can you help? What questions could you ask? What information could you share? Write down your thoughts below.

_____

_____

Tips for Older Children

- **Ask to see a picture of the person the child has lost.** Ask questions about the person. Ask them to share their favorite stories and memories.

- **Be inquisitive about the death.** Ask the child what happened. Ask how the child feels about what happened. Often, as a teenager tells their story, we can listen carefully for clues to what they are confused about or feeling guilty for.

- **Talk to your teenager about grief and the common emotions he/she is likely to feel.** If it is the child's first time with these intense feelings, they can be extremely frightening. Choose a book or two from the recommended resources list to help the teenager familiarize theirself with the emotions of grief. Look through the exercises in the *Difficult Emotions* chapter and share any you feel appropriate with the child.

- **Make a collage.** Help to gather magazines and pictures. Cut out words, pictures and notes that carry special memories. Place the finished collage in a place where the child can see it often. Consider framing the picture and hanging it in their room.

- **Help the child identify his needs and then relate them to others.** A teenager may feel unsupported, but it's hard for others to support him/her when they don't understand these needs. Identifying what would help most is a way to alleviate the unneeded pain of isolation.

- **Encourage or help your child to start a support group with other grieving friends.** Offer your home as a safe place to hold the meetings. Do whatever you can to help. Perhaps you could car pool and pick up other kids, provide snacks or beverages, photocopy handouts, etc.

Take a moment to think about your child. What information and support do they need from you? How can you help? What questions could you ask? What information could you share? Write down your thoughts below.

_____

_____

_____

_____

_____

_____

Chapter Seven
Special Occasions and Challenges

"Traditions are like rules; however well intentioned when it comes down to it, they were made to be broken. As children we lived for the opportunity to break rules and traditions, to strike out on a different path. Why not experience that joy? Change the meal, change the location, make new traditions; your life has changed tremendously and so should your traditions."—Scott Miller, Tips For Those Grieving During the Holiday Season

Holidays, birthdays, and other special days associated with the deceased, present a special challenge. The loss becomes painfully evident and the feelings associated with the occasion become dulled and gray. Try not to be alarmed by occasional setbacks. This chapter will give you some ideas and exercises about what to expect and what you can do.

Anniversaries

Some people find that they may do well for an entire year, only to find themselves virtually incapacitated by grief during the days surrounding the anniversary of the death. You wake up one morning with a heavy feeling, not knowing exactly why you feel so burdened. Then it hits you—the anniversary of one or another dates you shared with the deceased in the past.

On the anniversary of the day of death, many grievers report a short-term depression. It's not uncommon to experience discomfort, sadness and depression for a couple weeks before and after the date of death, each year. You may find some alternative solutions like herbs, vitamins and therapy to help you through this trying time. The strength of a support network can also be beneficial. Many people do "fine" throughout the year, only to be knocked off their feet as these significant dates occur.

Some religious traditions have a requirement around the one year anniversary of the death. In Judaism for instance, Judaic law has a prescribed ritual for "death days"—the anniversary of the death. You are expected to need to discharge extra emotions during these days. The headstone is unveiled at this time. Even if your religious tradition does not dictate it, you will feel some deep or extreme emotion on the anniversary of the death. Try to look at the anniversary of the death as another opportunity to grieve—to release some of what has been unexpressed up until now.

Other anniversaries where you can expect to feel "extra emotions" include:
- the last day you saw your loved one alive
- the day you first met
- the day you were married or engaged
- the day the "plug" was pulled

- the day you found out they were dead
- the anniversary of a trip you took together

Of course there will be others depending on your relationship to the deceased. If you expect these anniversaries to be challenging emotional times you will be less set back. If you identify these dates beforehand, you will be better able to cope. If you can, make special arrangements for yourself (i.e. take the day off from work, get a baby-sitter for the kids, find time and space to be alone, visit the grave, etc.) You may want to consider a ritual exercise below.

Rituals

Rituals are an important part of life. Through rituals we are able to observe, remember and structure our beliefs and feelings. In her book, *Surviving Grief,* Dr. Catherine M. Sanders writes, "In the past, rites of passage for every shift point in life were marked by rituals, which commanded a respected place in our culture. Large extended families came together to honor the person being celebrated. During chaotic times of change and transition, these rituals provided important direction and spiritual strength."

Funeral services are an example of a ritual. They give us guidance and direction that allow us to come together and celebrate life with those who share our loss.

Creating your own ritual may seem like a difficult task, but it doesn't have to be. To begin, ask yourself what you are trying to remember or celebrate. For many, a ritual on the anniversary date of the death is valuable. Others find they'd like to create a ritual for the birthday of the deceased. If the deceased was a spouse, the wedding anniversary may be a good time for a ritual. There are no limits on rituals. You can have one each season of the year, or one annually or every other year. Think about the purpose of your ritual as you decide on frequency. For most who are grieving, the ritual period becomes a time of breaking away from the day-to-day demands so we can experience our grief fully and focus on the memories we hold of our loved one.

Next, decide if you want the ritual to be just for yourself or if you want to share it with others. You may find that having a group of friends engage in the ritual is helpful. Others like this time to explore their emotions by themselves.

Where you should conduct your ritual is the next question to answer. There may be a special place that you associate with the deceased. You may want to stay close to home or you may wish to travel overseas. Again, keep your purpose in mind as you choose your location.

Below and on the following page you'll find rituals that those who we've known have conducted and found comforting.

Karen was living in France, when her mother died suddenly at the age of 50, leaving her father alone in the United States. Each year, Karen returns home for a week over the anniversary of her mother's death. She and her father use this time to r ecall their memories and visit the grave si te.

Jessica, Monica, Laura and Allie were close college friends, all living together. When Laura was killed suddenly in a car accident, the other three young women were torn apart. Each year, on the anniversary of the death, the three women get together and take a cruise. They recall their fun college days together. It has been five years since these women graduated and they still continue with this ritual.

David wanted to be alone on his deceased son's birthday. He rented a small cabin in the mountains and took nothing with him but spare clothes. He walked in the mountains, absorbed the beautiful scenery and "talked" to his son.

Cassandra, a single mother, was lost after the sudden death of her daughter. On the anniversary of her death, she asked her ex-husband to watch her other children. She took the weekend to write, cry, watch movies and look through old photos.

Which of the above ideas sounds comforting to you? Make a few notes of what would be comforting in your time of need. Take some quiet time to sit and think about what might help you to heal. Feel free to conform these rituals to suit your own needs, or to use them as sprinboards for your own ideas. Then commit to a ritual. Mark the dates off on your calendar.

_____

_____

_____

_____

_____

_____

_____

_____

_____

_____

_____

Holidays

With the loss of a member of your immediate family, holidays and special occasions will be difficult. Holidays are often filled with traditions and memories of closeness. As we face these days without our loved one, the empty space they leave behind looms large in our hearts. By creating new traditions and understanding the common difficulties faced during the holidays, they can be easier to cope with.

The American Association of Retired Persons offers the following tips in their article, "Frequently Asked Questions by the Widowed." (Italics, ours.)

Plan ahead. It helps to ease the strain.

Where will you be for the holidays?

_____

_____

Set priorities. This can make it easier to phase out elements less pleasing to you.

Are there any holiday activities you do not want to participate in?

_____

_____

Make new traditions. This new phase in your life deserves some new traditions.

What is a new tradition you could try? See the followingp page for additional suggestions and ideas.

_____

_____

Include [the deceased's] name in conversation. It helps others talk about him/her.
What story could you share with others this holiday season?

_____

_____

Express your feelings. Most people understand and accept your need to cry.

Find someone you can help. Giving assistance to others is very satisfying.

Who could you help this holiday season?

_____

_____

Buy yourself something special. You've suffered a great loss. Be good to yourself. *What special treat would you enjoy?*

_____

_____

Cherish your memories. They are yours to keep and grow more precious over time.

Be patient with yourself. Allow yourself extra time to accomplish tasks.

Take time out for rest and relaxation. This will ease the stress of grief.

Most importantly, take your time and be gentle with yourself as you move through the holidays.

Holiday Traditions

Don't try and hold on to the way things were done in the past or your previous traditions. Your family has changed. It's okay to change the way you celebrate the holidays as well. Think of a new tradition. If you always celebrated Christmas at home, consider renting a cabin for a couple of days. If you always put your tree up early in the year, consider putting it up later. If a large dinner was always cooked, go out for dinner instead. Do things differently. The memories will be strong when the holidays come; altering routines is the best way to still find some joy. Brook's family changed their routine after Caleb's death:

"Caleb died two months prior to Christmas. Both my mother and I had done most of our shopping. As Christmas neared and we were still heavily immersed in sadness, we wondered what to do with all the gifts. We decided to give them to Caleb's friends. To change our routine, instead of celebrating Christmas day at my mothers', she came down to my house in southern Wisconsin. Now, she comes out to my Portland home each year. While we always have Caleb in our minds and hearts, we have learned the need to let go of some of the pain and engage in activities and new traditions that can help us move forward with our lives. "

When we do what Brook has done we are honoring our lost loved one. It may seem as though we are disrespecting our loved ones or moving away from our memories—but in fact, we are paying tribute by moving on with our lives. Elizabeth was a newly widowed mother when the holidays came. She shares her story...

"The holidays, oh please save me from the holidays...make them go away! I remember my thoughts as a newly widowed mother of two young children sixteen years ago, as I raced around trying to put some kind of Thanksgiving and Christmas together. Can't we just forget about it this year? Doesn't the rest of the world know how much pain I'm in? I got together with another sad and lonely woman from my support group. I invited her and her kids to my house to have a turkey dinner for Thanksgiving. It helped to not face the carving of the turkey (which he did, rather poorly each year) alone. Somehow I did it, whatever "it" was, all the while listening to the happy Christmas carolers, fa la la la, la, la, la la.

Christmas day that first year was really strange. I opened the presents with my two children and then sat staring at the tree, imagining how it would feel to hurl the decorations off the deck and set the living room on fire. I must have sat in the green living room chair for two hours after that, not moving."

Where Does One Go During The Holidays?

Does one have to go anywhere? Do you have to pretend to be happy and joyous for the sake of others? Is it okay to celebrate this year if you want to? Like so much of the grief process, we need to listen to our inner guidance in these matters. If you need to be alone, that's okay. You can choose that. You may have to put something together for your kids and that's fine. You might find them a great joy , and inspiration, and a reason to get out of bed. Other than the practical needs of those who are dependent upon you, you don't need to take care of others by pretending "everything's all right."

If you do visit family and friends during the holidays, feel free to let them know the following ahead of time:

- I may need to leave your home earlier than you expect me to. (I get tired easily these days because I'm under a lot of stress.)
- I may need to take a walk by myself after dinner. (It's hard to be around happy families for too long a time.)
- I may cry unexpectedly when I hear certain music. (I have memories of good times and it's hard to hold back the tears.)
- I may not eat all the food and goodies you offer me. (My appetite hasn't been what it used to be—maybe I'm finding all this " hard to swallow.")

Even without a sudden death in your family or circle of friends, the holidays can bring up all kinds of difficult feelings. Depression is the most difficult feeling of all. You will need to face that it's going to be nearly impossible to stave off depression, especially at this time of year. Everyone seems to be so happy, families are gathering together, while there is a hole in your life. Walking through the mall you may see the perfect gift for your deceased loved one and dissolve into a flood of tears. You may have already bought the deceased gifts and there they sit, wrapped, under the tree, unopened. It would be extremely arrogant of us to suggest there is an easy fix for the kind of depression that surfaces around the holidays. Both of us, still suffer from periodic holiday blues. It may provide some relief to volunteer your time to help the needy and hungry. Giving of yourself to another, less fortunate person, or to someone who has experienced a similar loss, can take your mind off your own sadness—for a time.

This year, *you* be one of the first people you think about during the holiday season. A support group will be especially useful during this trying time of year. Peers can offer rituals and ideas they use to make the holidays easier, or they can offer a shoulder to lean on in your time of need.

What special needs do you anticipate having this holiday season after reading this chapter? What can you do in advance to ease holiday stressors?

_____

_____

_____

_____

_____

_____

_____

_____

Chapter Eight
Additional Exercises for Your Journey

"Let us turn over the page
And see what is written
On the other side of the night."
—Thomas McGrath, from *Graveyard Shift*

The exercises within this chapter cover a wide variety of situations and emotions. Read through them, finding those that pertain to your unique loss or will offer you comfort and growth.

Internalizing Our Loved One

The loss of a loved one takes an enormous toll on the soul. You may feel like their loss has taken a part of you away. One of the best ways to honor your relationship is to take some aspect of your loved one's life or the way he lived his life and incorporate this part of his personality into who you are.

Write about the traits you admired in your loved one. Choose one that you feel you could integrate into your personality as a tribute.

_____

_____

_____

_____

_____

_____

_____

_____

_____

Contributions in the Name of Someone You Love

Did your friend love children, lost animals, parks, the theater? Find an appropriate way to contribute time or money to an organization that promotes one of those special values.

List organizations you would like to research below.

_____

_____

_____

_____

_____

Helping Parents

If your loved one was the child of aging parents who cannot drive, or who may not be able to care for the grave site, assure them you will, with fresh flowers, weeding, etc. From time to time, take a photo of the grave site to show them.

What tasks might the parents need help with? What can you commit to helping with? Are there other people that you can solicit help from as well?

_____

_____

_____

_____

_____

_____

_____

Losing Our Parents

We expect to lose our parents—someday. We expect them to become frail and fragile and gradually "melt away" over time. And yet, few of us are really ready for our parent or parents to die, traumatically or suddenly. We believe there is "always tomorrow" to say what needs to be said, to express what we feel. There is always tomorrow to express the anger, the pain, the love and the gratitude. Then we are cut short, mission aborted and we are left holding a bag full of feelings that may be heavier than we can bear. The unsaid gratitude becomes outrage. The unexpressed anger turns inward and we are depressed. The unspoken pain they caused us becomes a stone we carry in our hearts or perhaps a guilt at the relief we feel in their passing. We were waiting for the "right time", but when sudden death occurs, the right time is gone.

Many of us look to our parents for guidance and acceptance well into our adult lives. We rely on their opinions. We rely on them for our roots. When we lose a parent, a part of our history disappears. We can no longer ask opinions or hear stories of when we were younger. We lose a piece of our foundation.

The next time you seek your parents advice, try writing to them. Ask them a question and then "write yourself back" imagining what they would say. When we live day in and day out with those we love, we become in tune to many of their responses and replies. When we find the stillness to listen, we can still hear. Use the space below and on the following page to write your parents and "listen" for their response.

Letter Writing Exercise

Write a letter to your loved one expressing your true feelings and place it in the casket before burial or cremation. If the body was not recovered, (or you are doing this exercise after the service) you can burn the letter on a beach or some other outdoor place. As the smoke rises, imagine the words are being carried on the air to your loved one.

Other Ideas to Honor Someone Who Has Died

Develop a Living Memorial

Many parents find comfort in developing a memorial, informational pamphlet or organization in their child's name. In our interviews we have found parents who have published information on drunk driving, drug use, suicide, gangs, etc. and distributed it in their local community, or sent it to newspapers around the country. Other parents have developed or founded organizations that are now national in scope. Other parents have found peace in starting a scholarship fund in their child's name and awarding the scholarship to a child who wants to pursue an interest similar to their child. Brook's family started an annual water-ski tournament in her brother's honor. Caleb was a nationally recognized water skier who enjoyed tournament skiing. Each year, they hold a tournament at the lake at which Caleb loved to ski, and award cash prizes and plaques.

International Star Registry

We discovered this group and thought the idea was precious. "Honor your loved one by giving them the stars! What a beautiful way to memorialize your child by naming a star after him or her! Since 1979, the International Star Registry has been bringing these dreams to earth by offering a unique and magical opportunity to name a star. Plus, when you purchase your star through MISS, a portion of the proceeds will be donated directly to the combined efforts of MISS and the Arizona SIDS Alliance." The star kit includes a certificate, a telescope coordinated for locating the named star, a large sky chart with the star circled for easy identification, an astronomy booklet and a memorial letter. The price ranges from $57-$106 including shipping and handling. For more information write to MISS/Star Registry, 8448 W Aster Dr., Peoria, AZ 85381 or visit the site online at http:// www.misschildren.org/family/starreg.html

Donations

In her book *A Handbook for the Living as Someone Dies*, Elizabeth A. Johnson suggests, "It may be very therapeutic and rewarding for you to donate your child's toys and other belongings to a children's home or to the children's wing at a hospital or hospice. In this way, the energy of your child's possessions is passed onto other children. A part of him continues to brighten the lives of others."

Memory Books

In *How to Support Someone Who is Grieving,* June Cerza Kolf writes, "Souvenirs, memorabilia and even some clothing can certainly be kept. In fact, putting old photographs in albums can be a task that is very rewarding at this time. It helps the bereaved recall happy memories."

Creating a memory book is a wonderful keepsake of our loved one. When Brook's brother died, she collected articles, photos and other memorabilia to put in a keepsake album. Using different papers, stencils, markers and stickers she created special pages to "frame" her memories.

Album making has become popular in recent years. Many scrapbooking stores now exist that offer classes on how to archive our memories creatively. Through collage, rubber stamping, paper decorations and other means, we can make a beautiful book to serve as a remembrance.

In addition to stores that can serve as creative outlets, many magazines and books offer guidance. Even if you don't consider yourself creative, there are tools to help you get started. Check the craft section of your local bookstore for books on scrapbooking. A large newsstand or craft store may carry magazines such as *Memory Makers* and *Somerset Studio*, which offer ideas.

There are also consultants for companies like D.O.T.S. and Creative Memories that both sell supplies and can help you choose supplies while offering creative guidance. Check your yellow pages for these companies. Current is another great source of materials. They can be accessed on the Internet at http://www.current.com

Here are a few basic tips for building your memory book:

1. Choose a good album to hold your memories. Creative Memories and D.O.T.S. both offer wonderful albums. Also make sure to use acid-free papers and supplies whenever possible. When papers are acid-free, they will not damage your photographs over time.

2. Collect all the materials that you think you would like to include. The possibilities are endless—postcards, words clipped from magazines, photos, special poems—anything that you like can be included.

3. Sort the items you have gathered until you see a natural progression take form. You may want to move through the book chronologically or another theme may occur to you.

4. Gather stencils, stickers, stamps and papers to use as decorations. Craft and scrapbooking stores are obvious suppliers. Additionally, office supply stores and stores like K-Mart, Wal-Mart and Target often have good selection at reasonable prices.

5. Choose the materials you would like to use for a given page. Lay them out and move them around until you are comfortable with the design. If you have problems coming up with ideas for layout, consult one of the aforementioned magazines.

6. Take your time. There is no need to rush through the process of creating a memory book. Many people find joy in the "putzing", the creating and remembering. It may be a book that you continually add to throughout your lifetime.

Visualization

Creative visualization can be a wonderful way to calm our minds and bodies. When our bodies are relaxed, we can play calming, healing and encouraging "movies" on the screens of our mind. These movies or imaginings can promote healing, forgiveness and peace.

Visualization may take a while to get used to. The first time you try it you may feel you aren't "getting anywhere." Give yourself some time. Like any exercise, visualization takes practice. Also, you may want to do your visualizations while laying on the floor or sitting in a chair. If you do them in bed, you could very likely fall asleep, since the process is e xtremely relaxing.

To begin, follow the whole-body-relaxation that is written about in the calming exercise. When your body is relaxed and you do not feel any excess tension, begin your visualization. As you do the exercises, thoughts and images may come to you that would be valuable to record. For this reason, it's a good idea to keep a visualization journal nearby.

Following are some visualization ideas. Choose one that feels comfortable to you or create one of your own. Feeding these positive messages into your mind will help reduce anxiety and depression—and help you to feel more joy and peace in life.

Visualize yourself using your grief in a creative way and a positive setting. Notice what you are doing, who is around you, how you feel and what you aare seeing.

What did you see during this visualization?

_____

_____

_____

If you feel guilt for the death, imagine blowing all the guilt within you into a balloon. See the guilt move out of your body, up through your lungs and into the balloon. See the balloon getting larger and larger until it contains all of your guilt. Hold on to the string of the balloon tightly, feeling all your guilt one last time. Then let it go. Watch the balloon carry the guilt away from you. You can use this same visualization with any other emotion that you want to get rid of—hatred, anger, jealousy or revenge to name a few.

How did you feel about the visualization?

_____

_____

_____

_____

Asking Questions through Visualization

If you want to communicate with the deceased or want to feel their presence, visualize them sitting in familiar surroundings. Go to them with your question or concern and let an exchange take place.

What question would you like to ask?

_____

_____

_____

_____

After your visualization, record your "answer".

_____

_____

_____

_____

_____

_____

_____

_____

_____

Visualizing the Future

Visualize yourself one or two years from now. Visualize the person you will have become and the positive changes you will have made. What comes to mind? Who is around you? What is your life like on a day-to-day basis? What do you believe in?

Record what you feel or visualize for your future:

_____

_____

_____

_____

_____

_____

_____

_____

_____

_____

_____

_____

_____

_____

_____

_____

Chapter Nine
Losing a Child

"O heart, hold thee secure
In this blind hour of stress.
Live on, love on, endure,
Though woe now jar the string
And all its music cease."
—Walter de la Mare

It has been said that there is no loss as devastating as the loss of a child. Sudden death is a mix-up of everything we know to be true in life. Losing a child to sudden death is a break in the natural law and order of life. The child we have spent our time loving and caring for and planning to watch well into adulthood, has been taken. It is a heartbreak like no other. Those who live through and survive such an ordeal without becoming bitter have the strongest, most loving souls of all people walking the planet.

In her book *Surviving Grief*, Doctor Catherine M. Sanders writes, "The reason parental grief is so different from other losses has to do with excess. Because loss of a child is such an unthinkable loss, everything is intensified, exaggerated and lengthened. Guilt and anger are almost always present in every significant loss, but these emotions are inordinate with grieving parents. Experts estimate that it takes anywhere from three to five years to reach renewal after a spouse dies, but parental grief might go on for ten to twenty years or maybe a lifetime. Our lives are severely altered when our child dies and there can be no replacement. Substitutes offer little respite. This is not to say that there is no hope for happiness. It is just that the shock and severity of this kind of loss leaves us feeling completely helpless and full of dark despair."

As Dr. Sanders has pointed out that our emotions will be intensified with the loss of a child. We have examined many of these emotions throughout this book—from guilt to anger to fear. In addition to these intensified emoitons, grieving parents find their relationships change or become strained. Let's examine the relationships of grieving parents in greater detail.

Your Relationship With Your Partner

The most intense stress to a relationship is the loss of a child. Studies have shown that married couples experience extreme stress during the three-year-period that follows the loss of a child.

Tonya lost her five-year-old son when he got in the crossfire of a robbery. She explains what she went through with her husband. "We were both so drained. It was like staring at each other through a thick fog—we kept trying to reach out to each other, knowing we needed each other, but we couldn't reach. He saw my pain and I saw his, and yet there was no energy to console each other."

Tonya's experience is a common one. A couple that previously worked as a team is left unable to function or help each other. The grieving process of couples is further complicated by history, gender differences and expectations.

In his book, *When Goodbye is Forever: Learning to Live Again After the Loss of a Child*, John Bramblett shares his experiences after the death of his son. One story exemplifies the differences within a couple. In this story, he and his wife were at a Rotary party. While discussing unusual events surrounding his son's death with a small group of people, he noticed his wife staring at him through the sliding glass door. He writes, "I knew what she was thinking; she knew what I was talking about. I wanted to communicate my experience; it was part of my way of coping. She felt that talking about those striking episodes in our family's life cheapened them. Neither of us was wrong; our approaches were just different."

Another complication is blame. If one parent was present when the death occurred, that parent may blame himself or the other parent may blame him. Blame creates guilt, conflict, anger and resentment. It is destructive and serves no purpose—yet it's a natural human emotion. One way we can combat blame-thinking is by putting ourselves in the other person's shoes. For example, if you are the one blaming your spouse—imagine how that makes your partner feel. If you are the one blaming yourself, imagine hearing a similar story from a friend. Wha t advice would you give him or her?

What complications or conflicts can you identify in you and your partner's relationship? Identifing problems instead of letting them build , can help resolve conflicts.

Grieving Styles:
The Differences Between Men and Women

Grieving within a couple is complicated further by gender differences. Men and women are taught to handle their feelings differently. Because of this, a woman may feel she is not being "heard or understood," when really her spouse is coping with grief the best he knows how. Likewise, a husband may feel he's not being heard because he is being pressured to talk or share uncomfortable feelings, when actually the woman is coping the best way she knows how.

Understanding the differences in men and women's grief is important for working through grief in a partnership. Here we will explore the common differences between men and women in the grieving process. By understanding these differences, we can become more open to other styles of grieving. Keep in mind that this section is written based on the majority of men and women, but there can be a great deal of crossover. These are general patterns that are not written in stone.

Terry Matine and Kenneth J. Doka offer the following summary in *Living With Grief After Sudden Loss,* "Masculine grief tends to be private, dominated by thinking rather than feeling, and action-oriented. While most masculine grievers are men, many women adopt this pattern of coping as well. Although traditional therapies have encouraged grievers to openly share their emotional distress and to recall painful events, masculine grievers may respond best to private, problem-solving approaches that respect and encourage emotional mastery."

Martin and Doka offer this outline as the usual masculine grief pattern. Reading this outline can help men identify their patterns and help those close to them create ways to work through the grief process.

- Feelings are limited or toned down
- Thinking precedes and often dominates feeling
- The focus is on problem-solving rather than expression of feelings
- The outward expression of feelings often involves anger and/or guilt
- Internal adjustments to the loss are usually expressed through activity
- Intense feelings may be experienced privately; there is a general reluctance to discuss these with others
- Intense grief is usually repressed immediately after the loss, often during post-death rituals

Which of the statements above relate to your partnership?

_____

_____

_____

_____

_____

Problem Solving Barriers

One of the main communication barriers is what men and women seek to get out of a conversation. Women seek someone to talk and explore with, whereas men often look to "solve the problem." Men will commonly put "solving and thinking" before "feeling and expressing." When faced with grief, a man may want to figure out how to support his family and how to be the anchor before exploring his feelings. Remember that many men believe they are responsible for taking care of the family. This belief makes it hard to show emotion when they feel they need to be providers. This is complicated further in many men by guilt. As the "protector" of the home, a man may feel guilty or that he has failed when his child dies. "I should have been able to protect him," is a thought that runs through the minds of many men.

Women are more apt to see relationships as the central point in their lives. Often, women's relationships and emotional ties to children and spouse come before any other need. When a child dies and the relationship is permanently severed, women often become introspective. Women worry less about the "outside world," and the logistics of "getting by," and more about life within the four walls of home.

How could you and your partner work around the problem-solving complication? Can you support each other's different needs for problem solving?

_____

_____

_____

_____

_____

_____

_____

_____

_____

_____

Guidelines for Grieving Men and their Partners

Ask Specific Questions

Men often aren't as familiar with their feelings and emotions as women. Questions like, "How are you feeling?" and "How are you doing?" are likely to be answered with, "I'm all right," or "Fine." It's not that men are avoiding answering the questions, they are simply answering them as they have in the past. Try more specific questions for more specific answers. Questions like, "What was the hardest part of the funeral for you?" "What do you think John would want us to do today?" will usually open up more conversation.

Allow Time

It may take a while for men to articulate how they feel. Keep in mind that most men have not had as many opportunities to articulate their feelings in a safe environment as women have. If a woman asks a question she needs to allow some time for the man to form his response. His reply could take a few minutes (or maybe even ten) but patience is key.

Start an All Male Support Group

Since men often grieve differently it can be valuable to start a support group that consists only of men. In the book Men and Grief (see Resources) there is a comprehensive section on how to start an all male support group.

Find a Physical Outlet

A punching bag, running, racquetball—anything physical can help release pent up emotion. When Brook's brother died, her mother wanted many things from the house thrown out. It had been years since they had completely cleaned the "very-lived-in" home. Brook's husband, Andy ordered a big dumpster to be brought in by a semi. Andy, and about ten other male friends of Caleb's, threw "everything" into the dumpster. They broke glass. They broke old doors. They vented. They cleansed. They purged. And in the end the dumpster was full of no longer needed clutter. The attic was clean, the basement organized and somehow their souls lightened. They had begun to let go. They had made order out of collected chaos. They had started the process of selected memory.

Give Men Space

Men don't like to "burden" others with their troubles. They may feel that grief is "their own problem" and that they should work through it on their own. Men may cope better by taking some time to "work through" their grief in a private setting. Since we all grieve differently and find different things helpful, it's best to be supportive of this need.

Guidelines for Grieving Couples

Read This Chapter Together

It's important that you both understand grief and how it affects you as a couple. Read and discuss this chapter together. Use it as a springboard for questions such as, "Do you experience that?" or "Would you like to try that?"

Find Additional Support

One mistake that many couples make in a marriage is the expectation of having all their needs met by one person—their partner. This is unrealistic and puts too much pressure on a partner. Our needs are so diverse, it takes a wide group of people to meet them. The same is true with grief. We need more than one person to help us through—we need diversity.

Discuss issues away from home.

The home environment will be charged with emotions and memories. To help overcome complicated emotions and distractions, make time to talk and share away from home. Go out for dinner. Go for a walk. Focus on one another and talk through joys, problems, pains and life.

Consider Letter Writing

In his column, Therapist Tom Golden, LCSW, advises, "One way to give men more time is to write to them, rather than talk to them. By writing a note it gives the man the freedom to read it more than once, to take it with him...and [more] importantly to respond in his own time. Another benefit is that writing takes the non-verbal communication and the "tone of voice" out of the equation. I know a couple that has a terrible time talking about their grief but when they start writing notes to each other they gain a greater understanding. Give it a try." (Tom Golden maintains an excellent web site, which has many articles on men and grief. Tom Golden: Crisis, Grief & Healing. See the Resources chapter for more information and the web address.)

Listen, Listen, Listen

For men, the job of "just listening" can be incredibly challenging. Men hate to see others in pain—they think that they should be able to prevent or "solve" the pain of their wife or loved ones. But it's important to remember that women need someone who will just listen. Practice listening at every opportunity you have. For women, listening involves paying close attention to non-verbal communication such as body language as well.

Convey Your Needs

Mis-communication is the number one problem in any relationship—from work relationships to friendships to marriage. Don't let miscommunication further complicate your grieving process. Don't expect your partner to know what you need—tell him specifically. Likewise, don't assume that you know what your partner needs—ask him specifically.

Compromise

Barbara D. Rosof offers this advice to couples, "In many areas of your life together, such as socializing, family activities, holiday observances, one of you will be more ready to reengage than the other. If your partner wants to do something and you feel unready, you may need to push yourself. There is a balance to be struck in your efforts. Your child and your loss will always be with you. But giving up your life with your partner and the pleasures you have had together will not lessen your loss. Your balance has to do with holding onto your child, yet finding a way to live your life for yourself and with your partner. Your balance will not be arrived at quickly. Expect false starts and uncertainty. You need your partner's patience and your own."

At some point, in order to effectively move forward, you will need to nudge one another and learn the art of compromise.

Stay Connected

Even though you are wrapped in your unique grief, do not give up your connection as a couple. Make time to spend with each other. Don't shut each other out or you will be strangers when you get to the other side of grief. Schedule at least 30 minutes a day to sit together. Try to talk to each other about your respective feelings and the challenges of the day. If you can't talk about that, try talking about memories. If talking is too difficult right now, just hold hands or hold each other. This daily communication, whether physical or verbal, let's each partner know that the other is committed to working through the tragedy—together.

Write down what you can do to communicate more and stay better connected.

_____

_____

_____

_____

_____

_____

_____

_____

_____

_____

Guidelines for Single Parents

Despite the difficulties in partner-grieving, grieving alone also carries its own challenges. Couples have each other to lean on, despite their grieving differences. Single parents, however, are emotionally isolated. While they may have a network of friends, or rely on their ex-partner for a sense of support during tragedy, the life-partnership found in couples isn't present.

Find Support
Don't try to shoulder all the responsibilities on your own. Instead, seek out a network of friends to help you. As a single parent, you might be used to tackling tough issues alone—but the loss of a child is too much to face by yourself. Let yourself lean on friends that make themselves available.

Learn to Ask for Help
Because you have handled so many things alone, it can be difficult to ask for help. You will need to push yourself to reach out during these difficult times.

Remember Your Ex is also Suffering
In the face of tragedy, try to put your differences with your ex aside. Respect that you are both grieving the loss of your respective relationship with your child. One of you may have had a stronger relationship, but that does not lesson the other parent's grief or make their grieving easier. Grieving for what "never was" is just as difficult as grieving for "what was"—perhaps even more difficult. (See the section on Multiple Grief.)

Living Children
Make sure to seek out another adult to help you care for surviving children during this time. They are experiencing their own grief, and although it can be easy to lean on them for support (especailly preteens and older), children need their own space to grieve and their own support network in which to do so.

Facing Your Loneliness
If you have lost your only child, you will likely experience a very intense sense of loneliness. At one point the title of "wife" or "husband" was taken from you and now you are forced to question your title as "mother" or "father". This is a very complicated mourning process and worthy of a book in itself. We strongly encourage you to seek the help of a professional if you face this identity crisis. We simply want to emphasize that parenting cannot be taken from you. Once you are a parent—you are always a parent.

When asked about family, Brook's mother always responds with, "I am the mother of two children—a living daughter and a deceased son. I couldn't have asked for better children, just a longer time to enjoy them both."

Chapter Ten
When Loss is from Suicide

"Gradually, I came to understand that while it may be possible to help someone whose fear is death, there are no guarantees for a person whose fear is life." —Carla Fine

According to a study released by the Center for Disease Control and the National Institute for Mental Health, suicide is the ninth leading cause of death in the U.S., with 31,204 deaths recorded in 1995. This approximates to around one death every seventeen minutes. There are more suicides than homicides each year in the United States. From 1952 to 1992, the incidence of suicide among teens and young adults tripled. Today, it is the third leading cause of death for teenagers aged 15-19 (after motor vehicle accidents and unintentional injury). Suicide is increasing, particularly for those under 14 and for those over 65. It is the third leading cause of death for people 15 to 24 years of age and is the sixth leading cause of death for children 5 to 14.

A 1991 U.S. Center for Disease Control Survey of high school students showed that 34% of girls and 21% of boys have considered suicide, actually *during the last year* 16% of high-schoolers made a "specific plan," 8% "tried suicide".

Suicide is one of the most devastating types of loss. In her book *How To Go On Living When Someone You Love Dies,* Therese A Rando, Ph.D. writes, "This can contribute to a profound shattering of your self-esteem, with strong feelings of unworthiness, inadequacy and failure. Like homicide, this death was not inevitable. It was preventable. You must recognize that you are particularly victimized by this type of death, and are susceptible to intensified and conflicted bereavement reactions."

But we are not at fault for someone's suicide. In the end, in the final moment, they made the choice alone. In *No Time to Say Goodbye: Surviving the Suicide of a Loved One,* Carla Fine writes, "Like most survivors, I was haunted by the infinite regrets that are woven into the fabric of suicide. I would replay the chronology of events leading up to Harry's death, searching for lost opportunities to reverse the inevitable outcome. Only as I began to accept the idea that my husband's choice to kill himself was his alone did the powerful grip of "what-ifs" of his suicide begin to loosen. Gradually, I came to understand that while it may be possible to help someone whose fear is death, there are no guarantees for a person whose fear is life."

Write about your feelings about suicide. What did you believe prior to experiencing a suicide of a loved one? What do you believe now? What questions do you have? Getting your feelings on paper is the first step in dealing with them.

Common Reactions to Suicide

Shock, guilt, grief, anger, depression and denial work overtime when someone commits suicide. Suicide is seen as a preventable death in the minds of many people. With this being the case many survivors feel intense guilt and anger since they were unable to prevent it. When the one who has died is your child, the emotions intensify further. The Compassionate Friends write, "The suicide of one's child raises painful questions, doubts and fears. The knowledge that your love was not enough to save your child and the fear that others will judge you to be an unfit parent may raise powerful feelings of failure. Realize that as a parent you gave your child your humanness — your positives and negatives — and that what your child did with them was primarily your child's decision. "

Questions and Suicide

"Why?" is the question that survivors of suicide ask over and over again. "Why would he (or she) take their life?" The "need to know" feelings are intensified when suicide occurs. The Mental Health Association in Waukesha County, Wisconsin published a pamphlet titled *Grief After Suicide,* which states: "Why would anyone willingly hasten or cause his or her own death? Mental health professionals who have been searching for years for an answer to that question generally agree that people who took their own lives felt trapped by what they saw as a hopeless situation. Whatever the reality, whatever the emotional support provided, they felt isolated and cut off from life, friendships, etc. Even if no physical illness was present, suicide victims felt intense pain, anguish and hopelessness. John Hewett, author of *After Suicide*, says, 'He or she probably wasn't choosing death as much as choosing to end this unbearable pain.' "

While you will never know the complete thought processes of the person who took his or her own life, know that you are not alone in your questioning. Many support groups, both in-person and via the Internet, can help you explore your questions and feelings. Please see the Resource Chapter for support ideas.

What questions do you have about suicide? Who could help answer them?

_____

_____

_____

_____

_____

_____

Religion and Suicide

There are many mixed emotions, thoughts and feelings on suicide and religion. For those affiliated with churches that take a harsh view of suicide, this can be an especially difficult time. In Eva Shaw's book, *What to Do When A Loved One Dies*, she writes: "While suicide is mentioned throughout the Bible's Old Testament, there is no opinion, condemnation or condoning. Saint Augustine said it was a grievous sin and the Catholic church and a few Protestant denominations have, at times, taken a harsh view of suicide. All major religions have abolished the philosophy that suicide is a cardinal sin, however, you may have to forgive [or ignore] a few people who make comments about the religious aspect of suicide."

The Compassionate Friends offer the following on the topic of suicide, "Cultural and religious interpretations of an earlier day are responsible for the stigma associated with suicide. It is important that you confront the word *suicide*, difficult as it may be. Keeping the cause of death a secret will deprive you of the joy of speaking about your child and may isolate you from family and friends who want to support you. Rather than being concerned about the stigma surrounding suicide, concentrate on your own healing and survival. Many parents prefer to use the phrase "completed suicide" rather than the harsh "committed suicide" when speaking about their child."

The people around us may also have a hard time understanding and accepting suicide. Therese A. Rando, PhD, writes, "The normal need to know why the death occurred will be intensified in suicide." You will need to work hard at answering the questions in your own mind, so that when you are ready, you can talk to others about your child comfortably.

If you have lost someone from suicide, get more information. The Internet has many valuable resources and online support forums; additionally, many books are devoted to the topic. If you are comfortable in a support group setting, there are many for suicide survivors. Check the Resource Chapter or call your local church, hospital or college for ideas on local groups. You will need to come to a point where you can remember your lost loved one realistically—both the positives and the negatives.

NOTES:

_____

_____

_____

_____

_____

The poem on the following page offers a beautiful perspective and ode to those we have lost from suicide.

Tattered Kaddish

by Adrienne Rich

Taurean reaper of the wild apple field
messenger from earthmire gleaming
transcripts of fog
in the nineteenth year and the eleventh month
speak your tattered Kaddish for all suicides:

Praise to life though it crumbled in like a tunnel
on ones we knew and loved

Praise to life though its windows blew shut
on the breathing-room of ones we knew and loved

Praise to life though ones we knew and loved
loved it badly, too well, and not enough

Praise to life though it tightened like a knot
on the hearts of ones we thought we knew loved us

Praise to life giving room and reason
to ones we knew and loved who felt unpraisable

Praise to them, how they loved it, when they could.

Singing Lessons

In *Singing Lessons* author Judy Collins writes about her personal journey of recovery after her son, Clark's suicide... "On the anniversary of Clark's death, I woke from a dream at midnight. In my dream I had been trying to persuade Clark not to die—striving to convince him that he didn't have to die, he didn't have to end his life. My son smiled and looked at me with love in his eyes. 'Mother...' he said, 'death is not an ending.' Today, I don't have to stay in depression. I know I have tools:

- I read a spiritual book
- I call a friend who has a kind word, a lift in her voice.
- I think about the good things in my life—often writing them down. There is so much in my life for which to be grateful.
- I smile with my husband, my friends, my mother and my sister.
- In the moment of silence, there is the sound of God bringing me strength—bringing me healing."

What tools do you have?

_____

_____

_____

_____

_____

_____

_____

_____

_____

_____

Chapter Eleven
The Loss of a Partner

"There is only one way for you to live without grief in your lifetimes; that is to exist without love. Your grief represents your humanness, just as your love does."—Carol Staudacher

The loss of a partner or spouse is devastating on many fronts. Our partner is often our confidant and best friend. We have both our emotional and physical highs and lows with this partner—day in and day out. To have this "half" taken away leaves us feeling incomplete, confused and shortchanged.

This is often intensified by the length of time we have spent with our partner. If we have been with our partner for many years, we may find that our partner completes our thoughts and is a compliment to our actions. We are left feeling as if we have lost half of our self in addition to our partner.

Added stressors arise at the life changes that often accompany the loss of a partner. We may have a significant financial change to endure, we may need to move, we may need to comfort our children and have few people to comfort us.

Loss of Identity

Our partner makes up a significant portion of our identity. Through and with our partner, we interpret the world, daily events and the ups and downs of life. When we lose this partner unexpectedly, we lose many of the foundations of our identity. We are left to rebuild at a time when we are both emotionally and physically depleted. This rebuilding process will take time.

Our friends and children may encourage us to move forward before we are ready. This is only to be expected, since those who care for us hate to see us in pain. Many people feel that by "getting back into life" our pain will be alleviated. These are good intentions, but this route does not work in reality.

As we grieve, we will need to rebuild our foundation one brick at a time. In his book *Loss*, John Bowlby writes, "Because it is necessary to discard old patterns of thinking, feeling and acting before new ones can be fashioned, it is almost inevitable that a bereaved person should at times despair that anything can be salvaged and, as a result, fall into depression and apathy. Nevertheless, if all goes well, this phase may soon begin to alternate with a phase during which the bereaved starts to examine the new situation and to consider ways of meeting it. This redefinition of self and situation is as painful as it is crucial, if only because it means relinquishing all hope that the lost person can be recovered and the old situation re-established. Yet until redefinition is achieved no plans for the future can be made."

At first, nothing will feel comfortable. Each day will bring new realizations and troubles. But in time, you'll find yourself engaging in a memory or hobby or thought that you enjoy. It may be only a minute of "peace," but it's peace nonetheless. This becomes your first brick. Seek out these sources of peace and record them in a journal. Notice what you like and what you don't. Form new opinions. Pursue a new interest. You may not be able to move quickly on these things. You may want to take a "getaway," but not have the emotional energy. That's fine. Order a few travel brochures on the Internet and page through them. A step is a step—no matter how small.

Write about the role you had prior to your loss and how that role has changed. What do you feel about it? Are you scared? Angry? Let your feelings flow.

_____

_____

_____

_____

_____

_____

_____

_____

_____

_____

_____

_____

_____

_____

_____

In Chapter 4, you'll find a Redefining Ourselves Exercise on page 46 that can help you in this process.

Some Things You Can Do

o As you move on with your life, remember this: The love you have for your deceased partner can always have a special place in your heart, even if/when you have another love relationship and/or remarry. Buy a special box for your momentos and revisit this box on special days if you want to.

o If no body was recovered, you may want to create a "burial place" and a memorial of some kind (perhaps donating a park bench or tree planting, etc. or burying a box containing photos or other personal items at a location you can visit).

o Donate time, money or special items to a charity that was important to your deceased partner.

o Incorporate some special trait or behavior of your deceased partner into your own life so that ev ery time you exhibit that trait or behavior, you will be honoring the loved one's memory.

o Place an "In Memory Of" ad in your local paper, in remembrance of your deceased partner and have it signify the closing of one phase of your life and the beginning of another. The ad can contain a favorite poem, song lyrics, special graphics or thoughts about your deceased partner. You can choose any date that was meaningful to both of you.

Which of these things could be of value to you?

_____

_____

_____

_____

_____

_____

_____

_____

Important Things to Remember on the Pathway

- **Grief knows no schedule.** Remember, if someone says something like, "It's time now to get on with your life," you have the right to say, "In my time and God's time, not in your time."

- **If you want to wear black you can.** You can also wear any other color you want during the time you are grieving.

- **If you need isolation for a while that is okay.** You will be with people when you are ready.

- **Find a safe time and place to "go crazy" if you want to.** Go yell in the woods, throw rocks at trees, swear at the TV or wear the deceased's clothes to bed.

- **Be kind to yourself.** Perfection is not necessary; there is no arriving, only going. There is no need to judge where you are in your journey. It is enough that you are traveling.

- **Make a commitment to your future.** Commitment enables you to bypass all your fears, mental escapes and justifications, so that you can face whatever you are experiencing in the moment.

- **Get out of your own way.** The main block to healing from loss is the thought that we shouldn't be where we are, that we should already be further along in our growth than we perceive ourselves to be. Let these expectations go.

- **Affirm yourself.** Who you were and who you will be are insignificant compared to who you are.

- **Your life has not been a waste.** Every individual in your life reveals a part of you that you need to encounter and serves as a medium, through which you can see yourself, grow in awareness and come closer to God within. Live every experience and every event you encounter as a learning opportunity, rather than as a threat of failure.

- **Fear is not always a bad thing.** If you allow yourself to experience fear fully, without trying to push it away, an inner shift takes place that initiates transformation.

There is no experience that exists in this life that does not have the power to lead you to greater knowledge and growth. Major loss can only become a vehicle for creating a renewed life when we stop thinking of it as a punishment and start to see it as a process. This process begins with the death of the relationship; proceeds through a period of grief and mourning, in which the death is recognized and accepted; and ends with a rebirth from our experience.

Chapter Twelve
Support Groups and Self-Help

"What is needed is an impossible situation where one has to renounce one's own will and one's own wit and do nothing but wait and trust the impersonal power of growth and development. When you are up against a wall, be still and put down roots like a tree, until clarity comes from deeper sources to see over the wall."
—Dr. Carl Jung

Survivors can feel isolated and may experience a resultant loss of identity. Some may experience not only the clearly defined stages in counselors' handbooks but also a lingering sadness. You may be aching for the deceased. Many people consult a pastoral counselor or grief therapist, but there are other sources—poetry, music, volunteer work, support groups, group therapy, self-help books and a variety of useful professional therapies which can frequently provide solace in unexpected ways. We have explored some of these in this chapter. One therapy or self-help avenue may work better for you than another. We all have unique needs and what will work best for you depends on your background and your belief system.

You may also want to work through this workbook with others. Sharing our experiences with one another can be a great step toward healing. In this chapter you will find some common forms of support and some exercises you can try.

On the following pages you'll find some valuable self-help exercises that can be done at any stage of the grieving process. You may want to purchase a special journal or blank book to record your exercises. It's important that you find a safe place to keep your writing so that you can write your true feelings, unobstructed. If you have small children, you may even consider a small safe. These are available at stores like Wal-Mart and Office Max and vary in price—but are affordable.

Many people find it helpful to create a writing ritual. Some people like to write upon waiting, others like to clear their head at the end of the day, and still others like to write both in the morning and evening. Experiment to find what works best for you. If writing daily is too much, write whena the spirit moves you. I encourage to you to try writing daily though—at least for a week or two. I think you'll find the benefits encouraging. Studies have shown that writing allows us to reach and unearth a part of us that we can't easily access through speaing with another person. After writing for several weeks, look back over your words—you will likely be surprised at what they reveal.

This section also contains answers to many of the frequently asked questions about self-help and therapy. This is a useful reference if you choose to seek professional help.

Journaling and Letter Writing

One of the most powerful tools for recovery is writing down your real thoughts and feelings in a journal—no editing or judgment. Writing a letter to the deceased can also be comforting. Some of your initial feelings will be quite strong or angry. Don't let this deter your efforts. You need to get those feelings out. After a while, your writing will turn softer as the emotional charge lessens. You have a unique and meaningful story to tell—the story of the beginning, middle and ending of a relationship. Telling your story, writing it in a journal, creating poems, hearing other's stories...these are some ways we heal. No one has to read what you wrote for this exercise to work, although you may want to read portions of your journal to your support group members. One woman I spoke with said, "What worked best for me was to keep a daily gratitude journal so I could see that my life was full of more than just grief and loss. It helped me feel more balance and gave me a perspective that was empowering."

In her book, *The Fruitful Darkness*, Joan Halifax reflects on our collective as well as personal stories when she writes, "Stories are our protectors, like our immune system, defending against attacks of debilitating alienation...They are the connective tissue between culture and nature, self and other, life and death, that sew the worlds together, and in telling, the soul quickens and comes alive."

In his classic book, *Reaching Out,* Henri Nouwen writes that though our own story "can be hard to tell, full of disappointments and frustrations, deviations and stagnations...it is the only story we have and there will be no hope for the future when the past remains unconfessed, unreceived and misunderstood."

Don't put any expectations or limitations on your writing—simply write. If you find it hard to get started, set a timer for five minutes and write anything that comes to mind. Don't stop. The writing may not make sense or be coherent, but it will help you get used to placing words on paper. Don't worry about spelling, grammar or style—just get the words out. Try doing a five minute writing exercises each morning when you awake or at night before going to bed. Try your first five-minute freewrite in the space provided below and on the following page.

_____

_____

_____

_____

_____

_____

_____

Freewrite continued...

Devotions and Journaling

For those of you who would appreciate guidance from the Bible in your journaling, there is a wonderful Internet site at GreifShare. The area is called "On Your Own: Daily Help and Encouragement". The area guides you to sections of the Bible that are relevant to the feelings, emotions and questions a person deals with during grief. The site offers 13 weeks of personal devotions. Each week contains five daily Bible studies and suggestions for further reading. Each day also has an "In Your Life" area, which asks you questions to help you identify where you are in your journey from mourning to joy. You can access this tool at http://www.griefshare.com

Take the time to find a way to tell your story. Listen to your story. Li sten to the stories of others.

Poetry

Poetry creates a bridge of feelings between the material world and the world of creativity and spirit. Visiting and/or joining a poetry group can have an extraordinary effect on the way we heal our grief. Poets, by definition, get to the raw feelings behind the masks we all wear. When we are wearing the mask of grief, we may feel that others cannot possibly know the pain we are experiencing, yet we must still continue living day to day in spite of our tremendous loss. As a result, we may feel out of touch with friends who have not experienced such a loss. We may feel that the strength of our feelings is unacceptable to others. Feelings are the dynamic force behind poetry groups. Within these groups you will find a welcome and sensitive home for the expression of your grief through the written and spoken word.

Search the World Wide Web for "Artists Salons" and/or "Poetry" in your state; also check your local paper for poetry readings. Attend the readings and ask participants about other local events in your area.

You can also write poetry on your own. Many books exist that can fuel creativity and offer guidance. Check the writing/reference section at your local bookstore. It can be extremely cleansing to spend a morning, once a week, at a cafe or park writing poetry in a beautiful journal. Don't worry about form—just creatively put down words to express yourself. Write poetry.

In the book, The *Poet's Companion: a guide to the pleasures of writing poetry,* authors Kim Addonizio and Dorianne Laux have a specific section on death and grief. They offer 10 suggestions for working with this subject. "Write a poem about a ritual that accompanies a death. It might be about a traditional funeral, a wake, or some more private or individual observance. If you find an occasion for the joy of beauty in the midst of mourning, include it." Another suggestion is, "If you own some object that used to belong to someone who is no longer alive, describe it in detail, along with your memories or images about how that person used it. You might also talk about how it is used in the present."

The Gratitude Journal

Sarah Ban Breathnach in her best-selling book, *Simple Abundance: A Daybook of Comfort and Joy*, advocates the use of a gratitude journal. She sites this as "a tool that could change the quality of your life beyond belief." We completely agree. This is how Sarah explains the gratitude journal:

> "I have a beautiful blank book and each night before I go to bed, I write down five things that I can be grateful about that day. Some days my list will be filled with amazing things, most days just simple joys. 'Mikey got lost in a fierce storm but I found him shivering, wet but unharmed. I listened to Puccini while cleaning and remembered how much I love opera.'
>
> Other days—rough ones—I might think that I don't have five things to be grateful for, so I'll write down my basics: my health, my husband and daughter, their health, my animals, my home, my friends and the comfortable bed that I'm about to get into, as well as the fact that the day's over. That's okay. Real life isn't always going to be perfect or go our way, but the recurring acknowledgment of what is working in our lives can help us not only survive but surmount our difficulties."

Recognizing the positives in our lives is especially important when we are engulfed in dark times. We often focus so heavily on our loss and what isn't going right, that we can't see any of the good things. For the first few months, it will be extremly difficult to find the positives, but after that initial time period, we need to begin looking again—no matter how simple these positives might be. Your list might include something as basic as "I was able to get out of bed today." What's important is that we be open to the fact that there are positives. By recognizing them, we attract more positives to our life.

For one week, keep your own gratitude journal recording five postiive things that happen each day. At the end of the week, write what you learned from this exercise. It will likely be on an activity you will want to continue!

Day One

_____

_____

_____

_____

_____

Day Two

_____

_____

_____

_____

_____

Day Three

_____

_____

_____

_____

_____

Day Four

_____

_____

_____

_____

Day Five

_____

_____

_____

_____

Day Six

_____

_____

_____

_____

_____

Day Seven

_____

_____

_____

_____

What I learned from the gratitude journal exercise:

_____

_____

_____

_____

_____

_____

_____

_____

_____

Frequently Asked Questions
about Self-help and Therapy

I know I need group support but what kind of group is best for me? How do I know which one is right?

A support or therapy group can be the ideal place for you to inexpensively explore your feelings. Your previous circle of mutual friends may no longer be available to you and a support group will be valuable in helping you re-establish your place in the world. Let's explore the basic group types.

A professionally led support group is organized and facilitated by a psychotherapist, pastoral counselor, psychologist, social worker or other mental health professional. You should feel supported and nurtured without judgment in this type of group. A fee may be charged since it is run by professionals.

A peer led support group is just that—led by someone who has experienced sudden death of a loved one and has decided to help others. Usually it is someone who is at least a year or two into the grieving process. There is normally no fee, or perhaps a donation will be requested of you .

A professionally led therapy group requires you to be in private counseling with the professional running the group and is an adjunct to your therapy work. You may also feel supported and nurtured in this group, but the therapist may challenge you on some of the beliefs you have that get in the way of your healing.

Many organizations form groups. Hospitals and religious organizations sometimes sponsor these groups. Therapists and social workers also form groups. Finding the right group for you will be easier if you pay attention to your intuition during and after the first meeting. At a time when we aren't sure of our ability to make decisions, trust your gut feelings to guide you. And don't give up, keep trying until you find the right fit.

Try the following exercise. The first time you go to a support or therapy group, take a pencil and paper with you. Either during or immediately after, jot down words that describe how you are feeling. Pay close attention to your feelings. Now do this again the second time you go, and once more on the third. Are you still feeling the same as you did the first time and second time? If your experience is mostly positive, continue with the group. If you notice you have written mostly about anxiety, fear, stress or shame, then stop going. Keep looking until you find a group that gives you positive feelings. Remember, a group is meant to be part of your extended support system. Take into account however, that you will not feel uplifted each time you go because the grieving process takes time and is full of its own ups and downs.

The stories of loss we have heard are as diverse as fingerprints—each one slightly different from the next. When we gather with those who attend and begin sharing, the connections, one to another, are astounding. Regardless of where we are in the process of grieving, or how we lost our loved one, we become supportive, relating and recognizing of each other's pain almost immediately. This sense of community and acceptance is vitally important to our spiritual and emotional healing.

On the following page, you'll find some questions that are useful for evaluating a support group.

Questions for a Support Group

These are some questions you will want to ask the person who is in charge:

Is there a fee? _____

How often do you meet? _____

Is there an attendance requirement? _____

Is it mandatory to share or speak at the group? _____

_____

How many people are there in the group? (If the group is larger than 10, you may not get your needs met as readily. There is only so much time for each person.)

_____

Is the group for men/women only? A group consisting of women only will help women develop supportive female relationships; and a group of all men will help men safely express their feelings.

_____

Allow the group the opportunity to "give" to you. Work on believing you have earned the right to receive. Don't be afraid to talk about or express your feelings. After all, that's why you came. You will not receive the support you came for if you hold back. Think about friends in your life and realize that it was with time that the level and depth of their friendship was revealed—the same is true in a group experience.

Use the following space to record information you learn about the support groups you talk to.

_____

_____

_____

_____

_____

_____

_____

Friends Support Group Invitation

The letter that follows is an example of a creative response to a need for support. The invitational letter was written to family and friends by the deceased's sister, Karen. Kathleen's death was a suicide which occured after a long struggle with cancer and mental illness. The letter was written on stationary with this quote imprinted in the corner: "What we call the beginning is often the end. To make an end is to make a beginning. The end is where we start from." -T. S. Eliot

Dear Family and Friends,

During the past few weeks I have had the opportunity to speak with some of you regarding the impact of Kathleen's death on your life. These discussions have served to assist me in dealing with my grief.

Some of you mentioned that you've been so busy that you've hardly had time to feel, much less deal with the loss. Many societies throughout the world have rituals built into their communities to facilitate the difficult walk through grief. Our "progressive" society has only begun to realize it's shortcomings, and in efforts to counter the emotional isolation, society has assigned the task of assisting us with our grief work to counselors and mental health care (bereavement groups). These are valuable, however, I'd like to propose that another helpful way might be for the members of Kathleen's community come together to talk, sit, just be together, in an effort to promote healing.

The nature of Kathleen's death has left us all with many questions. In discussing these issues with some of you privately, it has come up that talking about the issues together may assist us all in finding peace.

I have enclosed information our family received from the Albany Medical Center the night Kathleen died. We have found it helpful to review this information regularly in an attempt to monitor our healing.

If Kathleen had been a participant in a hospice program, they would be offering a program for bereavement for the family and friends to have a framework to evaluate progress along the grief walk. Her mental illness was indeed terminal. In an effort to create a structure for us to walk in our grief I'd like to host the following afternoon gatherings.

Also, my family is trying to piece together a historical outline of Kathleen's life, birth to death. We would find it helpful to hear your experiences with Kathleen so we can add them to the tapestry we hope to create.

Thank you all for taking the time to call and talk. I look forward to further discussions and insights.

Schedule of Bereavement Gatherings:

3:00-5:00pm at 134 Ridge Avenue
(for those of you who wish to stay after, soup and sandwiches will be served)

Saturday, January 27 -- 3 month anniversary of Kathleen's death
Saturday, April 27 -- 6 month anniversary of Kathleen's death
Saturday, July 27 -- 9 month anniversary of Kathleen's death
Saturday, October 26 -- 1 Year

The first year of feeling the void and figuring out ways to compensate is the most difficult. If you cannot attend these gatherings, I would request that you make time to remember the memories.

I'd appreciate an RSVP call.

For those of you who experienced Kathleen's association with the Native American culture, you may recall her referring to their custom of communication to "all my relations." This demonstrates the understanding that we are all part of a network, a web, a community. When the fabric of the web is broken, loose ends flap around until the members can come together and mend the space. How we choose to repair the hole will depend on who we are and what we will bring to offer each other. Thank you all for your willingness to offer and obtain comfort. The hope is that the memories which cause pain in the initial blow can, in time, serve as great comforts and a means for our own growth.

Blessings to all.
In light and love,
Karen

Use the space below to make your own notes for a family and friend support group invitation.

_____

_____

_____

_____

_____

Chapter Thirteen
Resources and Support

**"I give you what no thief can steal,
the memories of our times together:
the tender, love-filled moments"
—Edward Hays, Prayers for a Planetary Pilgrim**

In the following pages you will find a collection of resources to help you on your pathway of grief. Some of these are organizations that offer support groups that meet face-to-face. Others offer groups that meet online. Still other organizations offer newsletters, free brochures or magazines and many offer a combination of these services.

Some of these resources are available only via the Internet. Those resources are marked Internet Resource in parenthesis.

Supportive Publications

After loss
After loss provides a monthly newsletter on grief recovery. For more information write or call: 79301 Country Club Dr., Suite 1001, Bermuda Dunes, CA 92201; (800) 423-8811

Bereavement Publishing
Bereavement Publishing cares for the bereaved by providing resources. Bereavement Magazine functions as a "support group in print." They also offer a "Grief in the Workplace" program to help corporate America understand the needs of grieving employees. The group offers a magazine, 15 booklets, books, gift baskets and products, teaching tapes and a catalog. For more information write to Bereavement Publishing, 5125 N. Union Blvd., Suite 4, Colorado Springs, CO 80918.

Concern for Dying
After experiencing sudden loss, it is common for people to want to get their own affairs in order. The Concern for Dying organization provides resources that can help. *The Living Will* and *Durable Power of Attorney* are two documents that they will supply free upon request. Contact information: 250 West 57th Street, New York, NY 10107 or by calling (212) 246-6962.

One Caring Place
One Caring Place publishes many pamphlets dealing with difficult emotions such as grief, anger and loss. Brief and to the point, these caring publications offer wonderful support. You can contact them for a complete list of their publications by calling toll-free (800) 325-2511 or by writing to One Caring Place, Abbey Press, St. Meinrad, IN 47577.

The Centering Corporation

The Centering Corporation supports grieving people and those who care for and love them. They provide supportive resources for families, individuals, professional caregivers and friends. The organization was founded in 1978 and offers a free Creative Care Package Catalog. The catalog features over 200 books to support those experiencing grief or loss. You can request the catalog by calling (402) 553-1200 or by faxing (402) 553-0507 or by writing to 1531 N. Saddle Creek Road, Omaha, NE 68104.

Support for Loss of a Partner

American Association of Retired Persons – Widowed Persons Service

"The AARP Widowed Persons Service (WPS) is a community-based program in which trained, widowed volunteers reach out to the newly widowed. Established in 1973 and based on the 'Widow to Widow' research of Dr. Phyllis Silverman, WPS is a self help program offering one-to-one support, group work, public education, a telephone and referral service, and an outlet for rebuilding life as a single person. To locate the closest AARP Widowed Persons Service program in your community, call **1-800-424-3410** or e-mail griefandloss@aarp.org Additionally the AARP offers many helpful brochures including, *On Being Alone— A Guide for Widowed Persons, Final Details, Reflections and Suggestions on Making New Friends* and *When an Employee Loses a Loved One*. Their web site also contains comprehensive information, links and resources for dealing with grief. You can visit their web site at http://www.aarp.org They also hold online grief support chats three days per week on America Online. Visit their website for further details. You can write to them at 601 East Washington Street NW, Washington, DC 20049.

Death & Dying (Internet Resource)

This site offers comprehensive support for widows and widowers. They have a monthly newsletter that is delivered via e-mail and a moderated chat room. They also have message boards. Check out their offerings at http://www.death-dying.com

National Association of Military Widows

This group provides referral services for the newly widowed, sponsors social events and support groups, and lobbies for legislation beneficial to military widows. Contact them at 4023 – 25th Road North, Arlington VA 22207 or call (703) 527-4565.

Society of Military Widows (SMW)

This group serves the interests of women whose husbands died on active-duty, military service or during retirement from the armed forces. They can be contacted by e-mail at mconaus@aol.com or write to 5535 Hempstead Way, Springfield VA 22151 or call (703) 750-1342 ext 3007.

THEOS (They Help Each Other Spiritually) International

THEOS International has groups in both the United States and Canada that support widows and widowers. They also publish a magazine, book and organizational materials. For more information write or call: 1301 Clark Bldg., 717 Liberty Ave., Pittsburgh, PA 15222; (412) 471-7779.

The Beginning Experience

They offer international support programs for divorced, widowed and separated adults and their children, enabling them to work through the grief of a lost marriage. They can be contacted at 305 Michigan Avenue, Detroit, MI 48226 or by calling (313) 965-5110.

To Live Again

This mutual help organization is for widowed men and women who support one another through the grief cycle. Contact them at P.O. Box 415, Springfield, PA 15222 or call (412) 471-7779.

WidowNet (Internet Resource)

This is the most comprehensive site we've found for those who are widowed. WidowNet is an information and self-help resource created for, and by, widows and widowers. "Topics covered include grief, bereavement, recovery, and other information helpful to people, of all ages, religious backgrounds and sexual orientations, who have suffered the death of a spouse or life partner." You can access the site at http://www.fortnet.org/WidowNet/ They also have an IRC Chat. The group is most active on Tuesdays, Thursdays and Fridays after 8:00pm. To learn more about the group visit
http://www.fortnet.org/WidowNet/online/irc.htm

Support for Grieving Children

Camp "Good Grief"

Camp "Good Grief" is a summer camp program which offers grief education workshops and provides support and understanding for youth, ages 12-16, who have experienced the death of a sibling, parent, grandparent or close friend. The camp is held in New York. For more information visit the web site at http://www.campgoodgrief.com or write to The Good Grief Experience, Inc., 24 St. Bernard St., Saranac Lake, NY 12983.

KIDSAID (Internet Resource)

KIDSAID is an extension of GriefNet, a comprehensive Internet community that has provided support to over 3 million people in the last year. The KIDSAID area provides a safe environment for kids and their parents to find information and ask questions. To learn more about KIDSAID, visit GreifNet at http://www.griefnet.org

Motherless Daughters, Inc.

This national organization was founded in 1995 and now has 46 affiliated groups. They provide support, community and resources to women and girls who have experienced early mother loss. Information and referrals, national conferences, a newsletter, phone support and pen pals are available. Contact Motherless Daughter, Inc at Box 663 Prince St Station, New York, NY 10012 or call (212) 614-8047 or visit them online at http://www.dfwnet.com.md

Teen Age Grief, Inc.

Teen Age Grief, Inc. is a non-profit organization that provides expertise in providing grief support to bereaved teens. Their goal is to make grief support available to all teens from all walks of life in an environment that is accessible, safe and non-judgmental. Contact Teen Age Grief, Inc. at P.O. Box 220034, Newhall, CA 91322-0034 or call (805) 253-1932 or visit their web site at http://www.smartlink.net/~tag/index.html

RAINBOWS

RAINBOWS provides curriculum and training for establishing peer support groups for children, adolescents and adults who are grieving a death, divorce or other painful transition in their family. Contact this group at 1111 Tower Road, Shaumburg, IL, 60522 or call (800) 266 3206.

The Dougy Center for Grieving Children

This group, founded in 1982, offers two outlets—one for the region of Portland, Oregon and another that is national in scope. Through the National Center for Grieving Children & Families, this group offers support and training locally, nationally and internationally to individuals and organizations seeking to assist children and teens in grief. The mission of the Dougy Center for Grieving Children is to provide to families in Portland and the surrounding regions, loving support in a safe place where children, teens and their families, grieving a death, can share their experiences as they move through their healing process. You can learn more about these programs by contacting The Dougy Center for Grieving Children, P.O. Box 86852, Portland OR 97286 or call (503) 775-5683 or fax (503) 777-3097 or visit their web site at http://www.dougy.com

Support for the Loss of a Child

Aiding a Mother and Father Experiencing Neonatal Death (AMEND)

This organization strives to offer support and encouragement to parents grieving the loss of an infant through miscarriage, stillbirth or neonatal death. To learn more, write to 1559 Ville Rosa, Hazelwood, MO 63042 or call (314) 291-0892.

Alive Alone

Alive Alone is an organization for the education and charitable purposes to benefit bereaved parents, whose only child or all children are deceased, by providing a self-help network and publication to promote communication and healing, to assist in resolving their grief, and a means to reinvest their lives for a positive future. The group offers a newsletter subscription and special events. Contact information: website: http://www.bright.net/~alivalon/ e-mail: alivalon@bright.net, Address: Alive Alone, 11115 Dull Robinson Road, Van Wert, OH 45891.

Bereaved Parents of the USA

This national organization was founded in 1995 to aid and support bereaved parents and their families who are struggling to survive their grief after the death of a child. Information and referrals, a newsletter, phone support, conferences and meetings are available. They also offer assistance in starting a support group. You may contact them at P.O. Box 95, Park Forest, IL 60466 or by calling (708) 748-7672.

support, conferences and meetings are available. They also offer assistance in starting a support group. You may contact them at P.O. Box 95, Park Forest, IL 60466 or by calling (708) 748-7672.

Center for Loss in Multiple Birth (CLIMB)

This International network was founded in 1987 to support parents who have experienced the death of one or more of their twins or higher multiples during pregnancy, birth, infancy or childhood. They offer a newsletter, information on specialized topics, pen pals, phone support, materials for twin clubs and loss support groups. Contact them by e-mail at climb@pobox.alaska.net or by writing to P.O. Box 1064, Pamer, AK 99645.

Committee to Halt Useless College Killings (CHUCK)

This national network was founded in 1979 to support families who have lost a child to hazing or alcohol in fraternity, sorority or other college groups. They educate on the dangers of these practices and offer information, referals and phone support. Contact CHUCK at PO Box 188, Sayville, NY 11782 or call (516) 567-1130.

Hannah's Prayer

This International support group was formed to help those facing infertility, stillbirth and infant loss. They hold a Christian focus. You can contact them at: P.O. Box 5016, Auburn CA, 95604 or by calling (916) 444-4216.

Invincible Summer (Internet Resource)

Offers online e-mail support for those who have lost children. For more information e-mail jimncarol@earthlink.net

Meeting of Hearts (Internet Resource)

Two parents who lost their son tragically at the age of 20 founded this web site to offer others support. The site is beautifully done and offers a message board and valuable information. They also have a chat room. You can visit it at http://www.meetingofhearts.com/

Mothers in Sympathy and Support (MISS)

"The mission of Mothers in Sympathy & Support is to allow a safe haven for parents to share their grief after the death of a child. It is our hope that within these pages you discover courage, faith, friendship and love: The *courage* to speak out about your child and the love you have, regardless of the age or cause of death; The *faith* and reassurance that one day, we will all be reunited with our children—this time for eternity; *Friendships* with other families experiencing this tragedy; and finally, it is our hope that you discover the enormity and depth of the *love* you have for your child. A love that transcends time and distance; heaven and earth; life and death. MISS provides support to parents enduring the tragedy of stillbirth, neonatal death and infant death from any cause including SIDS, congenital anomalies, trisomy 13. Grief education for parents and professionals is our main focus. We must realize that the grief journey lasts a lifetime. Our child has changed our lives forever. Come with us and get lost in our pages...find healing, honesty, hope and a rediscovery of yourself." Visit this valuable web site on the Internet at http://www.misschildren.org/

Mommies Enduring Neonatal Death (MEND)

MEND is a nonprofit corporation whose purpose is to reach out to those who have lost a child due to miscarriage, stillbirth or early infant death and offer a way to share experiences and information through meetings, a bi-monthly newsletter and Internet web site. You may contact them at P.O. Box 1007, Coppell, TX 75019 or call (888) 695-MEND or e-mail bek4@ix.netcom.com

Mothers Against Drunk Driving

Mothers Against Drunk Driving is a non-profit grass-roots organization with more than 600 chapters nationwide. "MADD is not a crusade against alcohol consumption. Our focus is to look for effective solutions to the drunk driving and underage drinking problems, while supporting those who have already experienced the pain of these senseless crimes." MADD offers support groups and resources. You can search for a chapter near you on their web site at http://www.madd.org or by e-mail at Info@madd.org or contact their national office at P.O. Box 541688, Dallas, TX 75354-1688

National SIDS Resource Center

The National Sudden Infant Death Syndrome Resource Center (NSRC) provides information services and technical assistance on sudden infant death syndrome (SIDS)and related topics. Their goal is to promote an understanding of SIDS and provide comfort to those affected by SIDS through information sharing. NSRC's products and services include information sheets and other publications such as *What is SIDS, Sudden Infant Death Syndrome: Some Facts You Should Know,* and *Facts About Apnea and Other Apparent Life-Threatening Events*; Annotated bibliographies on SIDS and related topics from NSRC's databases, such as *Infant Positioning and Sudden Infant Death Syndrome, Smoking and Sudden Infant Death Syndrome, Children's Grief, and SIDS and Epidemiology*; Reference and referral services related to SIDS research, bereavement and public awareness about SIDS. To contact NSRC call, write, or e-mail: National Sudden Infant Death Syndrome Resource Center, 2070 Chain Bridge Road, Suite 450,Vienna, VA 22182, Phone: (703) 821-8955, Fax: (703) 821-2098, E-mail: sids@circsol.com Many of their informational sheets can be read online at: http://www.circsol.com/sids/

Parents of Murdered Children, Inc. (POMC)

Charlotte and Bob Hullinger in Cincinnati, Ohio founded POMC in 1978, after the murder of their daughter. What began as a small group, is now a national organization with over 300 chapters and contact people throughout the United States and abroad. The group provides the "ongoing emotional support needed to help parents and other survivors facilitate the reconstruction of a 'new life' and to promote a healthy resolution. Not only does POMC help survivors deal with their acute grief, but with the criminal justice system as well." The staff of the national headquarters of POMC will assist you, and if possible link you to others in your vicinity who have survived a loved one's homicide. In addition the staff can provide individual assistance and support. Should there be no chapter of POMC near you, they can aid you in starting one, if you wish. POMC also trains professionals in the fields of law enforcement, mental health, social work, community services, law, criminal justice, medicine, education and other fields that wish to learn more about survivors of homicide and the aftermath of murder. You may contact the National Headquarters at 100 East, Eighth Street, B-41, Cincinnati, OH 45202 or call (513) 721-5683 or fax (513) 345-4489 or e-mail NatlPOMC@aol.com or visit their web site at: http://www.metroguide.com/~world/pomc/info.html

Pen-Parents

Pen-Parents officially began its journey in April of 1988 in San Diego, California. Founder Maribeth Wilder Doerr, a bereaved parent, envisioned the need for a "pen-pal" network to help those who didn't feel comfortable with support group meetings or for those who lived in areas where traditional groups weren't available. The small kitchen-table operation has grown to over 800 members. This group serves as a support network of grieving parents who have experienced pregnancy loss or the death of a child(ren) through adulthood. They provide an opportunity for bereaved parents to talk about their child(ren) through a pen-pal type service by networking them with others in similar situations. You may write, e-mail, fax or visit their website at http://www.penparents.org, Email: penparents @penparents.org, Mailing Address: Pen-Parents, Inc., P.O. Box 8738, Reno, NV 89507-8738, Telephone: 702-826-7332, Fax: 702-829-0866.

Pregnancy and Infant Loss Center

The Pregnancy and Infant Loss Center offers referrals for bereaved families experiencing miscarriage, stillbirth and infant death. Contact them at: 1421 E. Wayzata Blvd., #30, Wayzata, MN 55391 or call (612) 473-9372.

Save Our Sons and Daughters (SOSAD)

SOSAD offers crisis intervention and a violence prevention program that provides support and advocacy for survivors of homicide or other traumatic loss. They offer weekly bereavement groups, professional grief counseling and training, education on peace movement to youth, advocacy, public education, a monthly newsletter, conferences, rallies and assistance in starting support groups. Contact SOSAD at 2441 W. Gran Blvd, Detroit MI 48208 or call (313) 361-5200.

SHARE: Pregnancy & Infant Loss Support, Inc.

This group offers support to those who have lost a child during pregnancy or infancy. Their extensive web site offers a chat room and many valuable reading areas. Additionally they offer a free newsletter. You can visit their web site at http://www.nationalshareoffice.com/ or you may contact them at: National SHARE Office, St. Joseph Health Center, 300 First Capitol Drive, St. Charles, Missouri 63301-2893, Phone: (800) 821-6819 or (636) 947-6164. All of SHARE's information packets, correspondence and support is free of charge for bereaved parents. They also publish a bi-monthly newsletter that is available to bereaved parents, free of charge for the first year.

SIDS Network: A World of Information and Support (Internet Resource)

This web site details Sudden Infant Death and Other Infant Death. Go to http://sids-network.org/ for an incredibly comprehensive and valuable web site. At last look, the site contained over 1000 files with information on, or related to SIDS. This is a very well done place for anyone seeking support or information about SIDS.

SIDS Alliance

The SIDS Alliance was established in 1987 in an effort to unite parents and friends of SIDS victims with medical, business and civic groups concerned about the health of America's babies. You can locate an alliance near you by visiting their web site at http://www.sidsalliance.org/family/ or by contacting their national office at (800) 221-7437 or write to Sudden Infant Death Syndrome Alliance, 1314 Bedford Avenue, Suite 210, Baltimore, MD 21208.

The Canadian Foundation for the Study of Infant Deaths - The SIDS Foundation

The Canadian Foundation for the Study of Infant Deaths is a federally registered charitable organization, which was incorporated in 1973 to respond to the needs of families experiencing a sudden and unexpected infant death. They offer some valuable brochures including: *Information about Sudden Infant Death Syndrome, When Your Baby has Died of Sudden Infant Death Syndrome, Having Another Child After a SIDS Death, Facts You Should Know About SIDS* and others. You may contact the resource by writing to 586 Eglinton Avenue East, Suite 308, Toronto, Ontario, Canada M4P 1P2 or by calling (416) 488-3260 or by faxing (416) 488-3864 or visit their web site at http://www.sidscanada.org/sids.html or e-mail: sidscanada@inforamp.net

The Compassionate Friends

The mission of The Compassionate Friends is to assist families in the positive resolution of grief following the death of a child and to provide information to help others be supportive. There are 575 Compassionate Friends chapters. You can locate the one nearest you online at http://www.compassionate friends.org/states.htm or for a chapter's contact number and meeting information call the National Office at (630) 990-0010 or fax (630) 990-0246. TCF also offers many helpful brochures. You can view them online at http://www.compassionatefriends.org/Brochures.htm The brochures cover many areas such as: *Understanding Grief When a Child Dies, Understanding Grief When a Grandchild Dies, The Grief of Stepparents When A Child Dies, When a Brother or Sister Dies, Caring for Surviving Children, How Can I Help When A Child Dies?, The Death of An Adult Child* and many others. TCF also publishes a magazine for $20 per year. You can subscribe to the quarterly magazine by contacting the national office. Contact information: The Compassionate Friends, Inc., P.O. Box 3696, Oak Brook IL 60522, Phone: (630) 990-0010, Fax: (630) 990-0246.

Trip's Heavenly Angels (Internet Resource)

Trip's Heavenly Angels is for parents who have lost a child or children through illness, accidents, miscarriage or stillbirth. An active and comforting online forum with chat rooms, message boards and more. Visit them at http://www.groww.com/Heavenly.htm

Unite, Inc.

This national organization, founded in 1975, has 14 groups. They offer support for parents grieving miscarriage, stillbrith and infant death. They have group meetings, phone help, a newsletter and an annual conference. For more information contact Janis Heil, Jeanes Hospital, 7600 Central Avenue, Philadelphia, PA 19111 or call (215) 728-4286.

General Bereavement Support

ACCESS: Air Craft Casualty Emotional Support Services

ACCESS provides comfort to friends and families of air disaster victims and survivors. ACCESS helps people cope with their grief and pain by connecting them to grief mentors who have also survived or lost loved ones in an air tragedy. ACCESS is there for as long as the grieving need support. They can be contacted at 1594 York Avenue, Suite 22, New York, NY 10028, (877) 227-6435. Or visit their website at www.accesshelp.org or e-mail info@accesshelp.org

Bereavement and Hospice Support Netline (Internet Resource)
This is a national online public service directory of bereavement support groups and hospice bereavement services. It's sponsored by the Hospice Foundation of America and the University of Baltimore. You can e-mail the group at bereavement@ubmail.ubalt.edu

Concerns of Police Survivors, Inc. (COPS)
This national assocation provides services to surviving friends and families of law enforcement officers killed in the line of duty. COPS can be contacted at PO Box 3199, Camdenton, MO 65020; or by calling (573) 346-4911 or by e-mail at cops@nationalcops.org

GriefNet (Internet Resource)
GriefNet is an Internet community consisting of more than 30 e-mail support groups and two web sites. Over three million people have visited the website in the last year. A very supportive site. Visit it at http://www.griefnet.org

Grief Share (Internet Resource)
This internet resource provides a comprehensive support group directory, special resources and a bookstore. Additionally, they have a wonderful area about journaling and a thirteen-week-guide with a Christian focus that includes scriptures, ideas for writing and journal pages you can print. Visit their site at http://www.griefshare.org

GROWW (Internet Resource)
GROWW is an independent haven for the bereaved developed by the bereaved. "At GROWW, you will find your partners in pain sharing their experience and strength. We have message boards, resource listings and secure chat rooms hosted by the most loving people on the Internet for all who are grieving." This site has a comprehensive chat schedule and great resources. You can visit it at: http://www.groww.com

Healing Hearts
Healing Hearts leads retreats, workshops and support groups that encourage individuals to explore their personal histories and gain insights and inner peace through the healing process. You may contact them at: (520) 219-8200 or by fax at (520) 219-8200. Or write to P.O. Box 65792, Tucson, AZ 85728-5792. Or you may e-mail them at grief@healinghearts.net or access their web site at http://www.healinghearts.org

Jewish Family and Children's Services (JFCS)
JFCS recognizes that today's fast-paced society does not offer most people the time, place or support to grieve fully when experiencing loss. JFCS has developed a comprehensive, non-sectarian bereavement program including counseling, support groups and educational workshops. JFCS bereavement specialists help people address their losses and experience new satisfaction in their lives. JFCS offers Widow and Widower Outreach and Support, Bereavement Workshops for those coping with the loss of a relative or close friend and individual and family counseling. They offer these services in three California locations. In

San Francisco call (415) 561-1212, in the Peninsula call (415) 326-6696 and in Marin County call (415) 507-0564. Or visit their web site at http://www.jfcs.org/bereavement.html

National Self-Help Clearinghouse

The National Self-Help Clearinghouse was founded in 1976 to facilitate access to self-help groups and increase the awareness of the importance of mutual support. The Clearinghouse conducts training activities for group leaders, carries out research activities, maintains a databank to provide information about and referrals to self-help groups, addresses professional and public policy audiences about self-help group activities, and publishes manuals, training materials and a newsletter. They offer many helpful brochures, and you can obtain more information by writing to the National Self-Help Clearinghouse at 25 West 43rd Street, Room 620, New York, NY 10036 or visit their website at http://www.selfhelpweb.org

National Organization for Victim Assistance

This organization promotes advocacy for victim's rights, offers help for crime victims and more. They also provide a 24 hour telephone crises service for victims. The hotline number is (202) 393 6682. To learn more about their resources, visit their web site at http://www.try-nova.com or write to 1757 Park Road NW, Washington DC 20010 or call Phone: (202) 232-6682.

Newsgroup alt.support.grief (Internet Resource)

Newsgroup allows users to post messages on the Internet and receive responses or respond to others. The alt.support.grief offers this opportunity to its users. With Newsgroup, however, it's always good to just watch and listen and get a tone for the group before jumping in with posts.

Remove Intoxicated Drivers (RID)

This national organization has 152 chapters in 41 states. Founded in 1978, this project is organized to advocate against drunk driving, educate the public and aid victims of drunk driving. You may contact RID at P.O. Box 520, Schenectady, NY 12301 or call (518) 372-0034.

Sena Webzine (Internet Resource)

Sena Webzine is dedicated to the enrichment of life through developing community awareness of grief and loss issues and promoting the recognition, understanding and support of those experiencing grief and loss. The magazine is a vehicle for the safe sharing of difficult and sometimes painful experiences in all stages of life. Overcoming fear through human compassion and caring involvement is the publication's objective. You can learn more about how to receive the webzine by accessing it online at: http://www.sena.org/v1i3masthead.html

The Growth House (Internet Resource)

Although this group's mission deals mostly with improving end of life care, their website has many resources that are valuable to anyone who is grieving. They also have specific pages on suicide. In addition, they offer a chat room. You can visit The Growth House at http://www.growthhouse.org

Thrive.Com (Internet Resource)

This well built Internet site offers many articles on grief and loss. They have an 'ask the expert' section, links to support, chat and resources. This is worth a regular visit for their regularly updated material. Access their site at: http://www.thriveonline.com/health/death/index.html

Tom Golden's Grief and Healing Discussions Page (Internet Resource)

This site uses a web message board where you can post and respond to issues of grief and loss. Access the message board at http://www.webhealing. com/cgi-bin/main.pl?

Tragedy Assistance Program for Survivors, Inc. (TAPS)

This is a national organization serving the families and friends of those who have died while on active military duty. You may contact them at 2001 S. Street, NW #30, Washington, DC 20009; or by calling (800) 959-TAPS.

Transformations (Internet Resource)

This well-designed site offers support in many areas, including grief. They offer a chat area and a schedule of events as well as a place to share your thoughts, stories, poetry and more. You can access the site at http://www.transformations.com/contents.html

Support for Loss through Suicide

American Association of Suicidology

The American Association of Suicidology is dedicated to the understanding and prevention of suicide. AAS promotes research, public awareness programs, education and training for professionals and volunteers. In addition, it serves as a national clearinghouse for information on suicide. Their web site also has a comprehensive listing of support groups. Simply click on your state for different groups. You can access this feature at: http://www.suicidology.org/survivorsofsuicide.htm
Contact information: 4201 Connecticut Ave., NW, Suite 408, Washington, DC 20008, Phone: (202) 237-2280, E-mail:ssilve16@ixnetcom.com

American Suicide Foundation

This national organization offers state-by-state directories of survivor support groups for families and friends of suicide. Contact them by e-mail at 76433.1676@compuserve.com or write to 1045 Park Avenue, New York, NY 10028; or call (800) ASF-4042.

Friends for Survival, Inc.

Organized by and for survivors, this non-profit group offers its services at no cost to those who have lost a loved one to suicide. Resources include a newsletter, referals to local support groups, a list of suggested resources and more. You may contact them at Friends for Survival, Inc., Post Office Box 214463, Sacramento, California 95821. Or call (916) 392-0664. They also have a Suicide Loss Helpline—(800) 646-7322.

Heartbeat

This support organization was formed for those who have lost a loved one to suicide. They offer referals to local support groups and information on starting your own group. You can write to them at 2051 Devon Street, Colorado Springs, CO 80909 or call (719) 596-2575.

Ray of Hope

This group offers information and resources related to suicide and information on starting your own support group. You can write to them at Post Office Box 2323, Iowa City, IA 52244. Or call (319) 337-9890.

SIEC (Internet Resource)

This is a comprehensive site for those looking to help someone with suicidal symptoms or who has lost someone to suicide. Many helpful and informative brochures can be ordered from the site and there are many stories shared as well. http://www.siec.ca/survivor.htm

suicide @ rochford.org (Internet Resource)

Suicide information and education. A very comprehensive source for those seeking to learn and understand more about suicide and its victims. Also lists many support groups.

Support for Siblings

Julie's Place (Internet Resource)

Julie's place is a web site that reaches out to grieving children and teenagers who have lost a sibling. They offer resources, a special remembrance area and many other valuable and comforting resource and communication opportunities for children. Access the site at http://www.juliesplace.com/

Twinless Twins

Twinless Twins is an organization comprised of nearly 1300 twinless twins that gather annually for a conference and encourage each other. Between conferences they telephone, write and e-mail each other. Many twins have found this communion with other twinless twins an immense help in their lives. If you are a twinless twin, call or write to: Twinless Twins Support Group International, 11220 St. Joe Rd., Ft. Wayne IN, 46835 or Phone: (219) 627-5414. You can also visit their web site at: http://serv1-r.fwi.com/twinless/

Suggested Reading

General books for adults:

A Time to Grieve: Meditations for Healing After the Death of a Loved One by Carol Staudacher, Harper SanFrancisco, 1994—365 daily readings offer comfort, insight and hope. This book is written specifically for people after the death of a loved one, however it is appropriate for anyone who still copes with the effects of a loss of any kind. A great gift for yourself or a grieving friend.

Beyond Grief by Carol Staudacher, New Harbinger Publications, 1987—This book is about understanding and then coping with loss, with clearly stated suggestions for each part of the grieving process. Written both for the bereaved and the helping professional, it combines supportive personal stories with a step-by-step approach to recovery. *Beyond Grief* acknowledges the path, reassures and counsels. Includes guidelines to create support groups and guidelines for helping others. It says to the grieving person: you are not alone, you can get through the pain, and there is a path back to feeling alive again.

Companion Through Darkness: Inner Dialogues on Grief by Stephanie Ericsson, Harperperennial Library, 1993—As a result of her own experience with many kinds of loss, the author offers an intimate, touching guide for those in grief. The book combines excerpts from her own diary writings with brief essays.

Complicated Losses, Difficult Deaths: A Practical Guide for Working Through Grief by Roslyn A. Karaban, Ph.D., Resource Publications 1999—Written by a pastoral counselor, certified grief therapist and death educator, the book deals with losses that are more difficult to cope with than others: suicide, sudden loss, the death of a child and murders among others---losses that evoke grief reactions and symptoms that are more intense and last longer than "ordinary" grief.

Dreams that Help You Mourn by Lois Lindsey Hendricks. Resource Publications, 1997--This book will put you in the company of other mourners and their dreams. You'll learn that dreaming after losing a loved one is absolutely normal. In fact, it's the soul's way of mourning. The book will help you take better advantage of the healing power of your dreams.

I Can't Get Over It: A handbook for trauma survivors by Aphrodite Matsakis, New Harbinger Publications, Inc., 1996—Explains how post-traumatic stress disorder (PTSD) affects survivors of a variety of traumas including disasters, rape, crime and violence. Addresses the survivor directly and helps them self-diagnose to then get appropriate treatment. Includes a variety of techniques and self-help suggestions for safe recovery.

In Memoriam: A practical guide to planning a memorial service by Amanda Bennett and Terence B. Foley, Fireside Books, 1997--Written in an easy-to-read format, this book provides a full range of options to help you choose music, arrange flowers, select a format, prepare a eulogy and invite speakers, and offers a wide range of selected appropriate readings.

Life After Loss: A personal guide dealing with death, divorce, job change and relocation by Bob Deits, Fisher Books, 1992—Provides skills for healthy recovery, including how to cry, how to write a goodbye letter, how to deal with emotions and how to cope.

Moving Beyond Grief: Lessons from those who have lived through sorrow by Ruth Sissom, Discovery House, 1994—A religiously oriented book offering stories of persons who have learned to cope with grief and trauma.

The Courage to Grieve by Judy Tatelbaum—This book covers many aspects of grief and resolution. Divided into five sections, it explores the grief experience and creative recovery.

The Dream Messenger: How Dreams of the Departed Bring Healing Gifts by Patricia Garfield. The author writes about the distinctive patterns that she discovered in her research of over 400 dreams. These include images of a journey, dream gifts from the departed, a "soul animal" whose characteristics are associated with the departed person, and images of a "veil" or boundary that separates the living the from the dead. She emphasizes that such dreams are an esential part of the healing process around mourning, providing comfort to the bereaved.

What to Do When a Loved One Dies: A practical and compassionate guide to dealing with death on life's terms, by Eva Shaw, Dickens Press, 1994—Presents excellent guidelines describing what to do when a death occurs. It has an extensive listing of support groups, resources and other sources of help. The approach is extremely detailed and includes sections on dealing with catastrophic deaths.

With Those Who Grieve: Twenty grief survivors share their stories of loss, pain and hope—by Kay Soder-Alderfer, Lion Publishing, 1994—Describes the healing process of grief and its effects, as well as how to find and offer help. The stories of grief cross the lifespans of these grief survivors.

Words to Comfort, Words to Heal: Poems and Meditations for those Who Grieve compiled by Juliet Mabey, Oneworld Publications, 1998—This lovely book would make a nice gift to give another or to give yourself. It features works drawn from poets, writers, philosophers and sacred literature. An inspirational anthology that celebrates lives that have ended and offers consolation to those left behind.

Books about Grief Recovery:

Grief's Courageous Journey: A Workbook by Sandi Caplan and Gordon Lang, New Harbinger Publications, 1995—Grieving the loss of a loved one is an intensely personal process. This workbook takes the hand of those who are left behind and guides them, at their own pace, along the path of their own healing journey. It provides a compassionate program for coping with day-to-day life and accepting the changes in yourself and others. Guided by a sequence of journaling exercises and suggestions for creating healing personal rituals, you can use the workbook to tell the story of your relationship with the person who died, grieve your loss and safely remember the past. You will also learn techniques for redefining your present life and re-creating your sense of future. The book includes a comprehensive, ten-session facilitator's guide for creating a grief support group in your community.

Healing our Losses: A Journal for Working Through Your Grief by Jack Miller, Ph.D., Resource Publications—The author shares experiences of loss in his own life and will guide you to record your memories, thoughts, and feelings about loss in your life. Journaling may be done alone or in a group setting.

Healing the Heart; Letting Go; Therapeutic Stories for Trauma and Stress; Stories to Heal the Grieving Heart (AUDIO TAPES), N. Davis, 1995, 6178 Oxon Hill Rd., Suite 306, Oxon Hill, MD, (301) 567-9297—These audio tapes contain collections of therapeutic stories designed to ease the process of grieving, explain stages of grief, address the intuitive side of the mind and help the listener find what he/she needs within the self. Visual imagery and relaxation exercises are also included.

Managing Traumatic Stress through Art: Drawing from the center by Barry M. Cohen, Mary-Michola Barnes and Anita B. Rankin, The Sidran Press, 1995—Provides step-by-step art experiences designed to help the reader understand, manage and transform the after effects of trauma. Written in a practical, useful style that shows the ways in which art-making and writing can assist one's healing from severe trauma.

The Grief Recovery Handbook by John W. James & Russell Friedman (Revised Edition), HarperCollins, 1998—Drawing from their own histories, as well as from others, the authors illustrate what grief is and how it is possible to recover and regain energy and spontaneity. Based on a proven program, this book offers grievers specific actions needed to complete the grieving process and accept loss.

Books for Grieving Men:

Griefquest : Men Coping With Loss by Robert Miller, St. Mary's Press, 1999—*GriefQuest* is a book of meditations written for men and the women who love and care about them. This book, written by other men, helps make sense out of the unique challenges that grief and loss force on men today.

Grief Therapy for Men by Linus Mundy, Abbey Press, 1998—This little book acknowledges the uniqueness of male grief and offers men real permission to grieve. It gives a host of practical suggestions for healthy male grief—what to do, what not to do, when to act boldly and when to just "be."

Men & Grief: a guide for men surviving the death of a loved one by Carol Staudacher, New Harbinger Publications, 1991—*Men & Grief* is the first book to look in depth at the unique patterns of male bereavement. Based on extensive interviews with male survivors, it describes the four characteristics of male grief, explains the forces that shape and influence male grief and provides step-by-step help for the male survivor.

When Men Grieve : Why Men Grieve Differently and How You Can Help by Elizabeth Levang, Fairview, 1998-- Insightful text on the unique characteristics of men's grief and how they face loss. Includes poetry and strategies for partners, friends and relatives.

Books about the Loss of a Friend:

Grieving the Death of a Friend by Harold Ivan Smith, Augsburg Fortress Publications, 1996--The death of a friend is one of the most significant but unrecognized experiences of grief in American culture. This unique new book moves with, rather than against, the natural grief process by exploring its many aspects-- the friending, the passing, the burying, the mourning, the remembering and the reconciling.

When a Friend Dies: A book for teens about grieving and healing by Marilyn E. Gootman, Ed.D., 1994, Free Spirit Publishing, Minneapolis, MN—A small, powerful book whose author has seen her own children suffer from the death of a friend. She knows first hand what teenagers go through when another teen dies. Very easy to read, some of the questions dealt with include: How long will this last? Is it wrong to go to parties and have fun? How can I find a counselor or therapist? What is normal?

Books about Helping Someone who is Grieving:

The Art of Condolence by Leonard M Zunin, M.D & Hilary Stanton Zunin, Harperperrenial Library, 1992—Offers specific and wise advice for responding to another's grief. Discusses what to write, what to say, and what to do.

When Your Friend's Child Dies: A Guide to Being a Thoughtful and Caring Friend by Julane Grant, Angel Hugs Publishing, 1998—A simply written, straight-forward book that will tell you what to say and do when you have a friend whose child has died. And, just as important, Chapter 1 tells you what not to say and why. An early reader described this book as a "slap-in-the-face wake-up call." After reading this book you will know how to comfort a parent who has lost a child, even ten years later.

You Can Help Someone Who's Grieving : A How-To Healing Handbook by Victoria Frigo, Penguin, 1996—A practical resource that deals with such issues as what to say and not to say after someone dies, how long the grieving period lasts and its many stages, how to write sympathy notes, and how to handle holidays and anniversaries.

Books about the Loss of a Child:

A Broken Heart Still Beats: When Your Child Dies edited by Anne McCracken and Mary Semel, Hazelden, 1998—Edited by two mothers who have each lost a child, this book combines articles and excerpts—some fiction, some nonfiction—that featured the death of a child. A brief introduction to each chapter, describes a different stage of the grieving process and how it affected their lives.

After the Darkest Hour the Sun Will Shine Again : A Parent's Guide to Coping With the Loss of a Child by Elizabeth Mehren, 1997—This inspiring guide to coping with the loss of a child combines the author's own story with the experiences and wisdom of others who have gone through this tragedy.

After the Death of a Child : Living With Loss Through the Years by Ann K. Finkbeiner, John Hopkins University Press, 1998—Drawing on her own experience with losing a child, an inspirational self-help guide for parents examines the continuing love parents feel for their child, ways to preserve the bond and strategies for coping with loss.

Recovering from the Loss of a Child by Katherine Fair Donnelley, Berkley Publishing Group, 1994—The death of a child is one of life's cruelest blows. This comforting book offers bereaved parents, siblings, and others inspiring firsthand accounts from people who have survived this heartbreaking experience. In addition to healing advice, the book illustrates how such deaths affect family relationships.

The Worst Loss: How families heal from the death of a child by Barbara D. Rosof, Henry Holt & Co., Inc., 1994—The death of a child overwhelms many people. This book describes the losses that the death of a child brings to parents and siblings, as well as potential PTSD reactions and work of grief. A very thorough and wise book. One of our favorite books on the topic.

When Goodbye Is Forever : Learning to Live Again After the Loss of a Child by John Bramblett , Ballantine, 1991—In 1985, John and Mairi Bramblett's youngest child, two-year-old Christopher, died in an accident, leaving them and their three older children devastated by shock and grief. Four months later, John began writing this deeply moving and honest story of how he and his family coped with the nearly unbearable pain of losing their son. *When Goodbye is Forever* walks us along the author's path to acceptance and recovery, taking us through the first hours and days of the tragedy, the painful but necessary first outings, and such occasions as Christopher's birthday, and the anniversary of his death. Mairi and the children share their responses to the tragedy as well, showing us the effect such a tragedy can have on the whole family.

General Books for Professionals:

Grief Counseling and Grief Therapy, 2nd Ed.: A handbook for the mental health practitioner, 1991, New York, Springer Publishing Company—Details ways to help clients accomplish tasks of mourning to avoid unresolved grief and its complications. A chapter on grieving traumatic losses is included, as are sketches for role-plays in training.

Helper's Journey: Working with people facing grief, loss and life-threatening illness by D. G. Larson, Research Press, 1993—Designed for volunteers, counselors and clergy who work in direct caregiving roles with survivors and those facing death. Gives practical suggestions as well as exercises and activities designed to develop coping skills.

Helping the Bereaved: Therapeutic interventions for children adolescents and adults, by A. S. Cool and D. S. Dworkin, 1992, New York, Basic Books—This professionally oriented book focuses on therapeutic interventions with bereaved individuals and groups. Gives therapists specific therapeutic techniques including development of ethical wills and rituals. It also addresses the development of groups for children and adults.

Living Beyond Loss: Death in the family by F. Walsh and M. McGoldrick (Eds.), W.W. Norton, 1995—This book aimed at professionals, looks at how the field of family therapy treats death and discusses the family impact of death and loss. It uses both systems and developmental perspectives.

The Many Faces of Bereavement: The nature and treatment of natural, traumatic and stigmatized grief by G. Sprang and J. McNeil, Brunner/Mazel, 1995—Written especially for professionals, this book provides an overview of traumatic grief and specific situations leading to traumatic grief (e.g. murder, critical incidents). It includes assessment protocols, debriefing strategies and treatment interventions.

Books for Children, Teens and their Caregivers:

A Taste of Blackberries by Doris B. Smith, Harpercollins Juvenil Books, 1992 (8-9 years)—The author conveys the experience and feelings of an eight-year-old boy whose best friend Jamie dies unexpectedly. The boy and his family, along with Jamie's family, deal with the myriad of questions and feelings engendered by this unexpected event.

Bart Speaks out: Breaking the Silence on Suicide (ages 4-12), by Linda Goldman, MS, Western Psychological Services, Los Angeles, CA—Bart, a lovable terrier, misses his owner Charlie, who has just died. But Bart's grief is complicated by the silence that surrounds Charlie's death. Sad and puzzled, Bart gradually comes to understand that Charlie has committed suicide. This workbook will give children an opportunity to explore suicide openly, to resolve their grief by breaking through the barriers of shame and secrecy that typically cloud this subject. Workbook exercises dispel myths about suicide, provide age-appropriate facts and explanations, and show children how to express their feelings.

Beat the Turtle Drum by Constance C. Greene, 1976, The Viking Press, NY (10-14 years)—In this touching story, the effect of the sudden death of an 11-year-old child on her older sister and parents is told with warmth and sensitivity.

Bereaved Children and Teens: A Support Guide for Parents and Professionals by Earl A. Grollman, Beacon Press, 1996—Explores the ways that parents and professionals can help young people cope with grief. Topics covered include what children can understand about death at different ages, the special problems of grieving teenagers, how to explain Protestant, Catholic, or Jewish beliefs about death in ways that children can understand, and more.

Breaking the Silence: A guide to help children with complicated grief by Linda Goldman, Western Psychological Services, Los Angeles, CA—Designed for both mental health professionals and parents, this book provides specific ideas and techniques to use in working with children who have suffered psychologyical trauma from violence, homicide, suicide or other traumas. Explains how to break the silence and then how to help children recover.

Coping with Death and Grief by Marge Eaton Heegaard, Lerner Publications, 1990—Includes stories about young people, grades 3-6, who deal with grief. Provides facts about death that are developmentally based.

Don't Despair on Thursdays! (ages 4-12) by Adolph Moser, Ed.D., Western Psychological Services, Los Angeles, CA—This gentle book lets children know that it's normal to grieve in response to loss and that grief may last more than a few days or weeks. Offers practical suggestions that children can use, day by day, to cope with the emotional pain they feel. Young readers will be comforted by the reassuring text and colorful illustrations.

Goodbye Rune (ages 5-11), by Marit Kaldhol and Wenche Oyen, Western Psychological Services, Los Angeles, CA—Rune and Sara are best friends, until the day that Rune accidentally drowns. This is a sensitive account of a child's first experience with death, Sara asks her parents endless questions, and their patient answers help her come to terms with the loss of someone special. She comes to realize that, through her memories, Rune will always be with her. Explores death and grief in terms children can understand.

Helping Bereaved Children, edited by Nancy Boyd Webb, DSW, Western Psychological Services, 1999—This book for therapists includes therapeutic interventions for children who have suffered a loss. Individual chapters focus on such topics as, death of a grandparent, father or mother, accidental sibling death, suicide of a parent, violent death of both parents, traumatic death of a friend, sudden death of a teacher, and more.

It happened to me: A story for child victims of crime or trauma,
Something bad happened: A story for children who have felt the impact of crime or trauma and All my feelings: A story for children who have felt the impact of crime or trauma by D. W. Alexander, 1992, Huntington, NY, Bureau for At-risk Youth—These coloring/workbooks are designed for early elementary school students. They identify the various components of PTSD and help with healing.

Life & Loss: A guide to help grieving children (Preschool through teen), by Linda Goldman, Western Psychological Services, Los Angeles, CA—Helpful information using photographs, children's drawings, essays, anecdotes and other simple techniques. Gives all the tools you need to help children through the grief process. Includes, how to recognize various kinds of loss, avoid blocked feelings, the four psychological tasks of grief, and how to commemorate loss among other topics. Offers a guide to community and national support groups and a list of materials addressing specific kinds of loss.

Lifetimes: A beautiful way to explain death to children by Bryan Mellonie & Robert Ingpen, Bantam Doubleday, 1987—A moving picture book for children of all ages that lets us explain life and death in a sensitive, beautiful way. With large color illustrations, it tells us that dying is as much a part of living as being born.

Part of Me Died, Too: Stories of creative survival among bereaved children and teenagers by Virginia Lynn Fry, 1995, Dutton Children's Books, NY—Eleven true stories about young people who experienced the loss of family members or friends in a variety of ways including, murder, suicide and accident. Includes writings, drawings, farewell projects, rituals and other creative activities to help children bring their feelings out into the open.

Straight Talk About Death for Teenagers: How to Cope with Losing Someone You Love by Earl A.Grollman, Beacon Press, Boston, MA, 1993 (13-19 years)—With reassurance and compassion, Grollman explains normal reactions to the shock of death, the impact of grief on relationships, dealing with pain, funerals, and much more. Includes a place for readers to record their memories.

Talking About Death: A Dialogue between Parent and Child by Earl A. Grollman, Beacon Press, 1991—How do you explain the loss of a loved one to a child? This compassionate guide for adults and children to read together features an illustrated read-along story, answers to questions children ask about death, and comprehensive lists of resources and organizations that can help. Helpful for children from preschool to preteen.

The Good Mourning Game by Nicholas J. Bisenius, PhD and Michele Norris, MSW, Western Psychological Services, Los Angeles, CA—Using an artistically designed game board, this resource is a wonderful therapy tool for children who've suffered a loss. The board illustrates nature's basic cycle, which, like the grief cycle, moves from stormy intensity to relative calm. It can be played by a therapist and one to three children in usually about 45 minutes.

The Grieving Child: a parents guide by Helen Fitzgerald. Fireside, 1992—Compassionate advice for helping a child cope with the death of a loved one. Also addresses visiting the seriously ill, using age-appropriate language, funerals, and more.

The Way I Feel: A story for teens coping with crime or trauma
It happened in Autumn: A story for teens coping with a loved one's homicide by D. W. Alexander, 1993, Huntington, NY, Bureau for At-risk Youth—These short books which include space for completing exercises, are part of a 6-volume series designed for teens exposed to crime and trauma.

What on Earth do you do When Someone Dies? (ages 5-10) by Trevor Romain, Western Psychological Services, Los Angeles, CA—Someone you love dies, and your whole world changes. Written to and for kids, this little book offers comfort and reassurance to children who've lost a loved one. It answers questions children often ask such as, Why? What next? Is it my fault? What's a funeral? It is still okay to have fun? Will I ever feel better? Includes a list of practical coping strategies.

When Something Terrible Happens: Children can learn to cope with grief (ages 6-12) and *When Someone Very Special Dies: Children can learn to cope with grief* by Marge Eaton Heegaard, Woodland press, 1992—These two books teach basic concepts of death and help children, through their workbook format, to express feelings and increase coping skills. Children use their own personal stories to complete the pages as they draw events and their accompanying feelings.

Books about the Death of a Mate:

How to Go On Living When Someone You Love Dies by Therese A. Rando, Ph.D., 1988, New York, Lexington Books—Includes suggestions for ways to deal with sudden or anticipated death. Offers self-help techniques to work on unfinished business, take care of the self and when to get help from others. Leads you through the painful but necessary process of grieving and helps you find the best way for yourself. Offers guidance to help you move into your new life without forgetting your treasured past.

Grief Expressed: When a Mate Dies by Marta Felber. Lifeword, 1997—This compassionate workbook guides you through the process of grieving the death of a mate. Sensitive writing and practical exercises help you to address issues such as loneliness, building a support system, managing sleepless nights, finances, self-nurturing and much more. The author has drawn from her own counseling background, as well as her self-healing after the death of her husband.

Widow to Widow: Thoughtful practical ideas for rebuilding your life by Genevieve Davis Ginsburg, M.S., 1995, Fisher Books—The author writes from her own experience as a widow and therapist. The book is frankly honest and attempts to dispel myths, disputes the rules and encourages the widow to begin her new life in her own way and time.

When Your Spouse Dies: A Concise and practical source of help and advice by Cathleen L. Curry, Ave Maria Press, 1990—This short book deals with a variety of practical topics within a spiritual framework. Includes topics such as advice on loneliness and sexuality, financial priorities and planning and good health practices, among others.

Living with Loss: Meditations for Grieving Widows by Ellen Sue Stern, 1995, Dell Publishing, NY—This book, small enough to fit in a purse, is full of supportive and empowering reflections. This daily companion is designed to help you cope today, cherish yesterday and thrive tomorrow.

Afterword

**"You don't get over it, you just get through it.
You don't get by it, because you can't get around it.
It doesn't 'get better'; it just gets different.
Every day... Grief puts on a new face..."
—Wendy Feiereisen**

The journey of grief is never one we want to embark upon, but sooner or later we are called to the path. For death and loss are just as much a part of this world as life and gain. It is in learning to understand and accept this cycle (even if we don't like it) that we begin to find our peace—and the solid footing needed to rebuild.

Tragedy catapults us into uncharted territory—a territory where we come face to face with unavoidable life forces. Lord Byron wrote, "Sorrows are our best educators. [One] can see further through a tear than a telescope." In times of tragedy we are given a new way of seeing the world and those around us. When we move through our grief, wading through its darkness, we can emerge with hope. This workbook serves as a guide for wading through that darkness. I strongly suggest coming back to these pages throughout the upcoming years. Your thoughts and responses may change as you acquire new perspectives with the passing of time. Perhaps the anniversary date of your loss would be the time to revisit this workbook and record what you have uncovered about the meaning of life—and the meaning of death.

I love the opening quote, written by my mother. She has summed up grief beautifully—"Every day... grief puts on a new face." We will always be touched by our loss, we are forever changed. Yet, we can choose to remember and honor our loved one. We can choose to keep memories, hopes and dreams alive and held closely in our hearts.

Each year, on my brother's birthday, my mother burns a candle for 24 hours. She reflects back on the joy of his birth—and the joy of his short life. Although there is a strong sense of sadness, she finds comfort in knowing he is embraced by the light of the candle, rather than shrouded in forgotten darkness.

As we live our lives, we can choose to become a light for those we have lost. We can carry their memory, their hopes, their dreams into the future. My co-author, Pamela D. Blair, says it well... "May you see light where there was only darkness, hope where there seemed nothing but despair, may your fear be replaced with faith and insight, may you feel some victory in the defeat and a sense of the sacred web into which we are all woven."

Brook Noel
August, 2003

Bibliography

Adrienne, Carol. The Purpose of Your Life Experiential Guide. William Morrow, 1999.

Akner, Lois F. Whitney, Catherine (contributor). *How to Survive The Loss of a Parent: A Guide for Adults*. Quill, 1994.

Albertson, Sandy. *Endings and Beginnings*. Random House, 1980.

American Association of Retired Persons Brochure, *Frequently asked Questions by the Widowed*.

American Association of Retired Persons Brochure, *On Being Alone*.

American Association of Retired Persons web site article, "Common Reactions to Loss."

Balch M.D., James F. and Phyllis A. Balch C.N.C. *Prescription for Nutritional Healing*. Avery Publishing Group, 1997.

Bowlby, John. *Loss: Sadness and Depression*. Harpercollins, 1980,

Bozarth, Alla Renee. *A Journey Through Grief: Specific Help to Get You Through the Most Difficult Stages of Grief*. Hazelden, 1994.

Bramblett, John. *When Goodbye Is Forever : Learning to Live Again After the Loss of a Child*. Ballantine, 1997

Breathnach, Sarah Ban. *Simple Abundance: A Daybook of Comfort and Joy*. New York: Warner, 1995.

Challem, Jack. "Relief for Chronic Fatigue: How NADH Can Help." *Let's Live*, October 1999. pp 48-50.

Chevallier, Andrew. *The Encycloped of Medicinal Plants*. Dorling Kindersley, 1996.

Childs-Gowell, Elaine. *Good Grief Rituals: Tools for Healing*. Station Hill, 1992.

Coffin, Margaret M. *Death in Early America*. Thomas Nelson, 1976.

Collins, Judy. *Singing Lessons : A Memoir of Love, Loss, Hope, and Healing*. Pocket Books, 1998.

Conway, Jim. *Men in Midlife Crisis*. Chariot Victor, 1997.

Curry, Cathleen L. *When Your Spouse Dies: A Concise and Practical Source of Help and Advice*. Ave Maria Press, 1990.

Cunningham, Linda. *Grief and the Adolescent*. TAG: Teen Age Grief.

Deits, Bob. *Life After Loss : A Personal Guide Dealing With Death, Divorce, Job Change and Relocation*. Fisher, 1992.

Doka, Kenneth J (editor). Kenneth, Kola J. (editor). Hospice Foundation of America. *Living With Grief After Sudden Loss : Suicide Homicide Accident Heart Attack Stroke*. Taylor and Francis, 1996.

Edelman, Hope. *Motherless Daughters: the legacy of loss*. Delta, 1995.

Editors of Prevention Health Books. *Prevention's Healing with Vitamins*. Rodale Press, 1996.

Ericsson, Stephanie. *Companion Through the Darkness : Inner Dialogues on Grief*. Harperperennial Library, 1993.

Flber, Marta. *Grief Expressed: When a Mate Dies*. Lifeword, 1997.

Fine, Carla. *No Time to Say Goodbye : Surviving the Suicide of a Loved One*. Main Street Books, 1999.

"Final Details." Brochure by The American Association of Retired Persons.

Fitzgerald, Helen. *The Mourning Handbook : The Most Comprehensive Resource Offering Practical and Compassionate Advice on Coping With All Aspects of Death and Dying*. Fireside, 1995.

Friedman, Russell and John W. James. *The Grief Recovery Handbook : The Action Program for Moving Beyond Death Divorce, and Other Losses*. Harpercollins, 1998.

Freud, Sigmund. From a letter to Ludwig Binswanger who had lost a son.

"Forgotten Mourners." The Journal News, July 29, 1999.

Fumia, Molly. *Safe Passage : Words to Help the Grieving Hold Fast and Let Go.* Conaris Press, 1992.

Ginsburg, Genevieve Davis. *Widow to Widow: throughtful practical ideas for rebuilding your life.* Fisher Books, 1995.

Grey, John. *Men Are from Mars, Women Are from Venus : A Practical Guide for Improving Communication and Getting What You Want in Your Relationships.* Harpercollins, 1992.

Grollman, Earl A. *Living When A Loved One Has Died.* Beacon Press, 1995.

Golden, Tom LCSW. "A Family Ritual for the Year Anniversary." Tom Golden Grief Column.

Goldman, Linda. *Breaking the Silence: A guide to help children with complicated grief.* Western Psychological Services.

Gootman, Marilyn. *When a Friend Dies: a book for teens about grieving and healing.* Free Spirit Publishing, 1994.

Goulston, Mark MD and Philip Goldberg. *Get Out of Your Own Way.* Perigee, 1996.

Halifax, Joan. *The Fruitfull Darkness: Reconnecting With the Body of the Earth.* Harper Sanfancisco, 1994.

Harris, Maxine. *The Loss That is Forever: The Lifelong Impact of the Early Death of a Mother and Father.* Plume, 1996.

Hays, Edward M. *Prayers for a Planetary Pilgrim: A Personal Manual for Prayer and Ritual.* Forest of Peace Books, 1998.

Heegaard, Marge Eaton. *Coping with Death and Grief.* Lerner Publications, 1990.

Hendricks, Lois Lindsey. *Dreams that Help You Mourn.* Resource Publications, 1997.

Henricks, Gay. *The Learning to Love Yourself Workbook.* Prentice Hall, 1992.

Hewett, John H. *After Suicide.* Westminster John Knox, 1980.

Johnson, Elizabeth A. *As Someone Dies: A Handbook for the Living.* Hay House, 1995.

The Journal News. "Forgotten Mourners: after the death of a brother or sister, family members often don't realize the extent of the siblings' grief." July 29, 1999.

Kennedy, Alexandra. *Losing a Parent: Passage to a New Way of Living.* Harper San Francisco, 1991.

King, Marlene. "The Surrogate Dreamers." *Intuition.* January/February 1998.

Kolf, June Cezra. *How Can I Help? : How to Support Someone Who Is Grieving.* Fisher Books, 1999.

Kubler-Ross, M.D., Elisabeth. *On Children and Death: How children and their parents can and do cope with death.* Simon and Schuster, 1997.

Kushner, Harold S. *When Bad Things Happen to Good People.* Avon, 1994.

L'Engle, Madeleine. *Sold into Egypt : Joseph's Journey into Human Being.* Harold Shaw, 1989.

Lerner, Harriet. *The Dance of Anger : A Woman's Guide to Changing the Patterns of Intimate Relationships.* HarperCollins, 1997.

Livingston M.D, Gordon. *Only Spring: On Mourning the Death of My Son.* Marlowe & Company, 1999.

Marshall, Fiona. *Losing A Parent: A Personal Guide to Coping With That Special Grief That Comes With Losing a Parent.* Fisher Books, 1993.

Matsakis, Aphrodite. *Trust After Trauma : A Guide to Relationships for Survivors and Those Who Love Them.* New Harbinger Publications, 1998.

Matsakis, Aphyodite. *I Can't Get Over It: A handbook for trauma survivors.* New Harbinger Publications, 1996.

Mabe, Juliet. *Word to Comfort, Words to Heal: Poems and Mediations for Those Who Grieve.*

Mechner, Vicki. *Healing Journeys*: The Power of Rubenfield Synergy. Omniquest, 1998.

Melrose, Andrea LaSonder (editor). *Nine Visions: a book of fantasies*. Seabury Press, 1983.

Mental Health Association in Waukesha County. "Grief After Suicide." Pewaukee, Wisconsin.

Miller Ph.D., Jack. *Healing our Losses: A Journal for Working Through your Giref*. Resource Publications.

Mitchard, Jacquelyn. *The Deep End of the Ocean*. Penguin, 1999.

Noel, Brook. *Shadows of a Vagabond*. Champion Press, 1998.

Noel, Brook with Art Klein. *The Single Parent Resource*. Champion Press, 1998.

Nouwen, Henri J. *Reaching Out : The Three Movements of the Spiritual Life*. Image Books, 1986.

Overbeck, Buz and Joanie Overbeck. "Where Life Surrounds Death." Adapted from Helpng Children Cope with Loss.

O'Neil, Anne-Marie; Schneider, Karen S. and Alex Tresnowski. "Starting Over." *People* magazine, October 4, 1999. p 125.

Prend, Ashley Davis. *Trancending Loss: Understanding the Lifelong Impact of Grief and How to Make It Meaningful*. Berkely, 1997.

Rando, Therese A. Treatment of *Complicated Mourning*. Research Press, 1993.

Rando Ph.D, Therese *A. How to Go on Living When Someone You Love Dies*. Bantam, 1991.

Rilke, Rainer Maria. *Letters to a Young Poet*. WW Norton, 1994.

Rosof, Barbara D. *The Worst Loss: How Families Heal from the Death of a Child*. Henry Holt, 1995.

Sachs, Judith with Lendon H. Smith. *Nature's Prozac : Natural Therapies and Techniques to Rid Yourself of Anxiety, Depression, Panic Attacks & Stress*. Prentice Hall, 1998.

Sanders, Dr. Catherine M. *Surviving Grief*. John Wiley, 1992.

Schiff, Harriet Sarnoff. *The Bereaved Parent*. Viking, 1978.

Shaw, Eva. *What to Do When A Loved One Dies: A Practical and Compassionate Guide to Dealing With Death on Life's Terms*. Dickens Press, 1994.

Staudacher, Carol.A *Time to Grieve : Meditations for Healing After the Death of a Loved One*. Harper San Francisco, 1994.

Beyond Grief : A Guide for Recovering from the Death of a Loved One. New Harbinger Publications, 1987.

Staudacher, Carol. *Men and Grief : A Guide for Men Surviving the Death of a Loved One : A Resource for Caregivers and Mental Health Professionals*. New Harbinger Publications, 1991.

Stearn, Ellen Sue. *Living With Loss : Meditations for Grieving Widows (Days of Healing, Days of Change)*. Bantam, 1995.

Stoltz PhD, Paul G. *Adversity Quotient : Turning Obstacles into Opportunities*. John Wiley & Sons, 1999.

Tatelbaum, Judy. *The Courage to Grieve*. HarperCollins, 1984.

Temes, Dr. Roberta. *Living With an Empty Chair : A Guide Through Grief*. New Horizon, 1992.

Viorst, Judith. *Necessary Losses : The Loves, Illusions, Dependencies, and Impossible Expectations That All of Us Have to Give Up in Order to Grow*. Fireside, 1998.

Webb, Denise, Ph.D. "Supplement News." *Prevention*, October 1999. p 61.

Westberg, Granger E. *Good Grief*. Fortress Press, 1971.
Zarda, Dan and Marcia Woodaard. *Forever Remembered*. Compendium, 1997.

Worwood, Valerie Ann. *The Fragrant Mind*. New World Library, 1996.

Zunin M.D., Leornard M. and Hilary Stanton Zunin. *The Art of Condolence*. Harperperrenial Library, 1992.

TO CONTACT THE AUTHORS...

Send an e-mail to media@championpress.com
Please indicate which author you are writing in the SUBJECT LINE

Or write to:
Brook Noel or Pamela D. Blair
c/o Champion Press
4308 Blueberry Road
Fredonia WI 53021

**To order additional copies of this book,
please mail the order form below to**

Champion Press, Ltd.
4308 Blueberry Road
Fredonia W I 53021

Or call 262.692.3897 or visit www.championpress.com
to order with your credit card

By Brook Noel and Pamela D. Blair, Ph.D.
I Wasn't Ready to Say Goodbye Companion Workbook _____ x 18.95 = _____
I Wasn't Ready to Say Goodbye – Main Book _____ x 14.95 = _____

By Brook Noel
GriefSteps: 10 Steps to Rebuild, Recover and Renew _____ x 18.95 = _____
    after any life loss – Companion Workbook
GriefSteps: 10 Steps to Rebuild, Recover and Renew _____ x 14.95 = _____
    after any life loss – Main Book
The Single Parent Resource _____ x 13.95 = _____
Back to Basics: 101 Ideas for Strengthening Our Children _____ x 13.95 = _____
    and our families

Audio CD's by Brook Noel
Helping Children Cope with Grief _____ x 14.95 = _____
I Wasn't Ready to Say Goodbye (abridged) _____ x 14.95 = _____
Surviving the First Few Weeks _____ x 14.95 = _____

GriefSteps (abridged) _____ x 14.95 = _____

Subtotal
WI residents add 5.6% sales tax _____
Shipping 3.95 for the first item, $1.00 for each additional _____
Priority shipping add $5.00 in addition to the above shipping figure _____
Grand Total _____